Who Will Teach?
Policies That Matter

Richard J. Murnane, Judith D. Singer, John B. Willett,
James J. Kemple, and Randall J. Olsen

Harvard University Press
Cambridge, Massachusetts
London, England
1991

Library of Congress Cataloging-in-Publication Data

Who will teach? : policies that matter / Richard J. Murnane . . . [et al.].
p.   cm.
Includes bibliographical references and index.
ISBN 0–674–95192–1 (acid-free paper)
1. Teachers—United States—Job satisfaction—Evaluation.
2. Teachers—United States—Certification—Evaluation.   3. Murnane, Richard J.
LB1775.2.W48   1991
371.1′0023—dc20
91–2324
CIP

#23180136

In memory of Francis Keppel, whose life's work was important to American education, and who was a supporter of this project from its inception

Contents

Acknowledgments

A great many people contributed to the research project that led to this book. Richard Berry of the National Science Foundation (NSF) was instrumental in securing initial funding for our five years of research. Ron Anderson of NSF helped us to obtain supplemental funding to support creation and analysis of national data sets. We are grateful to them and to the National Science Foundation for their continued support. We also appreciate the support of the Spencer Foundation, which provided funding for the research underlying Chapters 2 and 3.

Engin Konanc and Brock Murray of the North Carolina Department of Public Instruction and Robert Carr and James Phelps of the Michigan State Department of Education provided critical data sets and answered innumerable questions.

Barbara Beaudin, Michael Schwinden, Joseph Shivers, Dennis Sweeney, and David Title, while students at the Harvard Graduate School of Education (HGSE), participated in the herculean task of creating final data sets from the dozens of computer tapes provided by state departments of education. Their doctoral work using these data sets provided many ideas that are reflected in this book. Greg Davidson provided skilled research assistance during the early part of the project.

John Hahnfeld, the director of the HGSE computer center, was consistently supportive of our computing efforts, despite the problems that our large data sets created. He worked with us effectively to find solutions to the many computing problems that arose during our work. Anne Chase and Beth Gamse provided critical help with the data cleaning and programming required to create national data sets of college graduates from the National Longitudinal Surveys of Young Women, Young Men, and Youth. Jane Gerloff typed multiple drafts of each chapter, mastered Harvard Graphics, and made many revisions of the figures included in the book. She did this with a rare mixture of efficiency and good humor that made her a delight to work with.

The following people read parts of the manuscript and gave us helpful comments: Barbara Ankeny, Joan Baratz-Snowden, David Cohen, Allan Collins, Ed Doherty, Carol Dwyer, Richard Elmore, Pascal Forgione, Eric Hanushek, Harold Howe, Mary Kennedy, Stephen Klein, Michael Lipsky, Patrick Murnane, Barbara Neufeld, Edward Pauly, Vito Perrone, and Brian Stecher. Judith D. Singer thanks the National Academy of Education for its support during her Spencer Post-Doctoral Fellowship. We would also like to thank Angela von der Lippe and Elizabeth Gretz of Harvard University Press for their interest in our book and their help in bringing it to publication.

Finally, we would like to thank our families for their encouragement and support.

January 1991

Who Will Teach?

1

The Teaching Profession at a Turning Point

In the 1990s, America's public schools will hire more than two million new teachers.[1] This number is larger than the total number of accountants, lawyers, judges, and physicians working in the United States in 1988,[2] and represents a 35 percent increase over the number of new teachers hired between 1980 and 1990.[3]

Why such increased demand for teachers? The answer lies in demographics. Today's teachers are aging, and each year, more and more of them, especially those hired during the baby boom years of the 1950s and 1960s, are retiring. At the same time, after years of decline, public school enrollment is growing as the "baby boomlet"—the *children* of the baby boom generation—enters school. Between 1990 and 2000 public school enrollment will increase by 8 percent, to 44 million.[4]

Will there be enough teachers to teach these children? This question attracts a great deal of attention each September as the media report predictions of teacher shortages. Past experience indicates that somehow enough teachers will be found to staff the nation's schools. But there is a more pressing question: Who will these teachers be?

America is worried about its teachers. Each year, a new blue-ribbon commission issues another report examining America's schools, decrying the declining quality of the teaching force and predicting further problems ahead. Some stress the growing need for qualified mathematics and science teachers able to keep abreast of increasingly complex technology. Others point to the diminishing numbers of Black and Hispanic teachers, particularly when the number of students of color is growing. All call for attracting bright and energetic college graduates into the profession—men and women who know their subject matter well, who can communicate their knowledge to others, who can stimulate young people to learn, and who will continue to learn more themselves. In the words of the Carnegie Forum on Education and the Economy: "[T]he key to success lies in creating a profession equal to the task—a profession of well-educated teachers prepared to assume new powers and responsibilities to redesign schools for the future . . . [T]he teaching profession is the best hope for establishing new standards of excellence as the hallmark of American education."[5]

Such concerns about teachers are hardly new. Over seventy years ago, the National Education Association argued that "the teaching profession must be made attractive to the ablest men and women of this generation. Public schools must afford opportunity to render service untrammeled by needless annoyances and obstacles. Teaching service and teachers should command the respect and challenge the admiration of every community where public schools exist."[6] Decades of rhetoric have not raised the profession's status in the United States. Today, as earlier, teaching remains an occupation with relatively low salaries and even lower prestige.[7]

What will happen to our schools if these conditions continue as the demand for teachers rises? We have little doubt that college graduates will be found to staff the nation's classrooms, just as they were in the 1960s, during the last "teacher shortage." Few classes will be canceled for lack of a warm body at the front of the room. But without significant changes in policy, the next generation of teachers will increasingly be those college graduates with the poorest alternative career options. Bright, well-educated graduates will seek and obtain opportunities in other fields, leaving the weakest graduates to teach our children. The quality of teaching will suffer generally, but the quality of instruction in certain subjects, including chemistry and physics, will be particularly hard hit. Classes in these areas will be taught by individuals with minimal training in the subject, because graduates well prepared in these fields will be drawn to high-paying positions in business and industry. Thus, during the decade in which the President and the nation's governors promise to achieve the goal of making American students the best in the world in science and mathematics, the nation's schools will be staffed with teachers lacking the skills to respond to this challenge.[8]

But this bleak forecast of the future of the nation's schools need not come to pass. The prediction assumes a continuation of past policies, which, as discussed in Chapters 2 through 6, discouraged many talented college graduates from teaching. Policy changes, however, described in

Chapters 7 and 8, can enable the nation's schools to attract and retain talented teachers.

Carrots and Sticks

Prompted by widespread concern about the quality of the teaching force, legislators have turned to perhaps the most obvious approach for making teaching more appealing: higher salaries. Between 1980 and 1988, the average starting salary (net of inflation) for a new public school teacher, fresh out of college with no experience, rose by almost three thousand dollars, to $19,600.[9] Whether these salary increases have been large enough to influence the composition of the teaching force has not been clear because, prior to this book, there has been little research on this question. What has been clear, however, is that state and local tax increases are needed to fund such salary increases.

As taxes have been raised to pay the bill for teacher salary increases, many state legislators have worried that higher salaries, by themselves, will not produce a better teaching force. This concern has led many state legislatures to link salary increases to policies aimed at raising standards for the teaching profession. They have used two approaches: requiring that new teachers have more education, and raising the passing scores prospective teachers must attain on standardized multiple-choice tests— most commonly, the NTE tests (formerly known as the National Teacher Examinations). Each approach has strong and vocal proponents. Schools of education, many of which are part of large state universities, have a vested interest in maintaining their role as gatekeepers to the profession. And the appeal of testing to the public is obvious. We want our students to know more—why not turn the tables and demand that teachers know more?

But these two approaches will not raise standards and may even, if continued, lead to disaster. They will produce a talented teaching force only in wealthy communities able to pay extremely high salaries. Most other communities will find themselves facing an even weaker applicant pool. Why? Because increased training requirements dissuade many academically talented graduates from entering teaching. This leads to shortages of qualified teachers and creates enormous pressure for exceptions, which undermine the attempt to raise standards. Raising the minimum passing scores on the standardized multiple-choice tests used in many state licensing systems presents a different problem. It does not improve the teaching skills new entrants bring to the classroom, but it does reduce the number of minority group members who become teachers. Taken together, these popular policies aimed at improving teaching will fail to achieve their goal. As this failure becomes evident, public support for teacher salary increases will diminish, and the old status quo will return: teaching will again be a low status, relatively low paying occupation, perceived to be the occupational choice only of those with no better option.

The flaw in conventional approaches to raising standards is that they are blind to their effects on the career choices of teachers and potential teachers. Making it more difficult to become a teacher will not produce a more skilled teaching force unless teaching is a desirable career choice. To date, it has not been.

The key to designing a successful strategy for improving the nation's teaching force is to recognize that the people we would most like to teach our children are college graduates with the best alternative career options. To attract them into teaching, we must adopt policies that increase the attractiveness of teaching relative to other occupations.

How can we predict which policy initiatives will most influence the career decisions of potential teachers, current teachers, and former teachers? Until now, policymakers have had little choice but to rely on untested conventional wisdom. Few studies have examined the effects of salaries in teaching, of salaries in other fields, or of teacher licensing requirements on the career decisions of college students and teachers. When data have been used to support policy proposals, the most compelling evidence has come not from studies of teachers' career choices but from survey responses given by current and former teachers questioned by the National Education Association and the Metropolitan Life Insurance Company.[10] The surveys of former teachers paint a particularly stark picture. Over the course of several administrations of these surveys, former teachers consistently report that their current work lives are more satisfying and less stressful than were their previous teaching jobs, and that they are paid better in their current jobs and are just as satisfied with their health and retirement benefits. Over 80 percent say they are unlikely ever to teach again.[11]

Although these surveys describe former teachers' *perceptions* of why they left the classroom, we believe that asking people retrospectively about the reasons for their job changes cannot tell us whether policy changes, such as raising salaries, will affect the career decisions of present and future teachers. We adopt a different research strategy and examine whether prospective teachers, current teachers, and former teachers who face different incentives make different career decisions. By studying responses to the many "natural experiments" that differences in salaries and licensing requirements provide, we identify incentives and obstacles that influence career choices.

In this book we present findings from quantitative analyses of the career decisions of over fifty thousand college graduates who considered teaching in the 1960s, 1970s, and 1980s. The data come from the nation as a whole and from two states, North Carolina and Michigan. The national data are drawn from the National Longitudinal Surveys of Labor Market Experience, and are described in Appendix A. They document important changes over the last twenty-five years in the characteristics of college graduates who enter teaching. We find that changes in opportunities, especially for Black college graduates and women, have influenced career choices. We constructed the state-specific data sets from information provided by the state Departments of Education in Michigan and North Carolina. In examining the career patterns of teachers in the two states, we focus on those hired during the early 1970s, the most recent period of relatively stable enrollments. As explained in more detail in Appendix A, this period was chosen because student enrollment patterns affect career decisions. Since today's critical policy questions concern teachers' career decisions in the 1990s, when enrollments will be growing, the most reliable evidence comes not from recent years, when enrollments were declining, but from the last period of relatively stable enrollments. The evidence from Michigan and North Carolina demonstrates that teachers working in different parts of the country, in states with quite different economies, respond similarly to differences in teaching salaries and to differences in opportunities outside of teaching.

Critical Questions

In examining the career decisions of college students and teachers, we pay particular attention to the evidence on four critical policy questions: (1) Do dollars make a difference? (2) Can we find enough mathematics and science teachers? (3) Are we losing the brightest? (4) Why are there fewer and fewer Black teachers?

Do dollars make a difference?

Teacher salaries in the United States are determined locally by each of the nation's fifteen thousand school districts. Most districts specify a base salary for a teacher with a bachelor's degree and no experience, and salary increments for each advanced degree and year of experience up to a prespecified maximum.[12] Typically each teacher in a district is paid according to the same schedule, regardless of grade level or subject taught.

During the last twenty years, the purchasing power of teachers' salaries has fluctuated widely. The average starting salary (expressed in 1988 dollars) peaked in 1973 at $20,400. Over the next decade, salaries fell behind inflation, so that by 1981, the average real starting salary had fallen by 18 percent to $16,700. Although the purchasing power of salaries in other occupations also fell during the 1970s, teaching salaries declined relative to salaries in many other occupations during this period. For example, in 1973, college graduates trained in mathematics who became teachers earned, on average, 77 percent as much as graduates trained in math who entered business or industry. The comparable figure for 1981 is 65 percent.[13] Prompted, in part, by widespread concerns about the quality and quantity of teachers, salaries increased steadily during the 1980s, so that by 1988, as already noted, the average starting salary was $19,600, an increase of nearly $3,000 since 1981, but still almost $1,000 below the 1973 level.

Do teachers' salaries affect career decisions? Do these career decisions affect students? Most research has focused, not on these questions, but on the more general question of whether educational expenditures are associated with educational quality. The debate on this issue has been intense, partly because the evidence is mixed. Advocates of increased expenditures for teachers specifically, and schools in general, point to the problems caused by today's fiscal austerity—forty students crowded in a classroom, leaky roofs and broken windows, textbook shortages, no extracurricular programs, no chalk. Without additional expenditures, they argue, America's schools will deteriorate even further.[14]

Supporters of tax limitation, by contrast, draw upon research showing no systematic relationships between expenditures and student learning. They cite, for example, the work of Eric Hanushek, a noted economist who has studied this topic extensively. He concludes that "[t]he available evidence suggests that there is no relationship between expenditures and achievement of students, and that such traditional remedies as reducing class sizes or hiring better trained teachers are unlikely to improve matters."[15] If greater spending does not guarantee more highly educated students, the argument goes, why spend more money?

Much of the debate about school expenditures has been sterile because it ignores *how* dollars are used. Researchers have not carefully analyzed how spending money in one way or another does or does not affect students' experiences. They have not traced how differences in districts' budgets affect who teaches in our schools.

We explore two mechanisms through which expenditures affect who teaches and where. First, we examine how fiscal resources affect school district hiring practices. Adequate funding levels can facilitate creative solutions to the challenges districts face in hiring skilled teachers. Second, we show that salaries make a difference in how long teachers stay in the classroom. Better-paid teachers stay in teaching for longer periods of time, and the effect of salary is especially pronounced during teachers' early years on the job. In Chapter 8 we explore how policymakers can use these findings to redesign teacher compensation policies.

Can we find enough mathematics and science teachers?

The publication of *A Nation at Risk,* the report of the National Commission on Excellence in Education, focused national attention on American students' dismal performance in mathematics and science. The symptoms are certainly alarming: American schoolchildren perform so poorly on standardized tests of mathematics and science achievement that they often come in last when compared with students from other industrialized countries; College Board achievement test scores in physics and mathematics continue to decline, as they have for years; over one quarter of the mathematics courses taught in four-year colleges are remedial, covering subjects usually taught in high school.[16] Will our schools ever produce a technologically literate and numerate work force?

The roots of America's problems in mathematics and science are deep and complex, but one contributing factor may well be school districts' inability to recruit and retain sufficient numbers of highly skilled teachers trained in these areas. Although researchers disagree about whether there are currently shortages of mathematics and science teachers,[17] it is clear that improving the mathematics and science achievement of American students will require finding greater numbers of skilled math and science educators.

Why do schools find it so difficult to hire and hold on to skilled teachers in these fields? In the early 1960s, Joseph Kershaw and Roland McKean argued that the problem lay in the structure of public school salary schedules.[18] Their argument is elegant and persuasive. People generally take jobs offering the highest salary available to them. Teachers' low starting salaries are especially unattractive to college graduates trained in mathematics and the sciences because they can command much higher starting salaries in business and industry. As long as school districts ignore differences in teachers' backgrounds and training, talented college graduates with technical skills will take jobs elsewhere.

This argument would be weak if we were talking about small salary differentials, but we are not. The salary differentials between jobs in education and jobs in the private sector have been, and remain, large (Figure 1.1). In 1988, when the average starting salary for teachers was

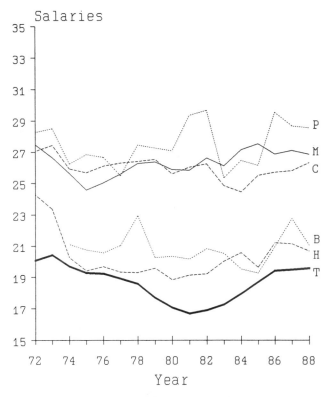

Figure 1.1   Starting salaries (in thousands of 1988 dollars) by field (P = physics; M = math; C = chemistry; B = biology; H = humanities; T = teaching). (Teacher salaries from the American Federation of Teachers; starting salaries for graduates taking jobs in business or industry from College Placement Council surveys.)

$19,600, business and industry offered average starting salaries of $28,900 for physics majors, $25,900 for chemistry majors, and $21,000 for humanities majors.[19] Teaching jobs have always been less lucrative than jobs in business and industry, but the salary gap is especially pronounced for those trained in mathematics and science. A $2,000 salary differential might be acceptable if accompanied by flexible workdays and summers off; an $8,000 salary differential is probably hard for any college graduate to swallow.

We build upon Kershaw and McKean's argument by exploring differences in teachers' career decisions by grade level and subject specialty. Teachers' career paths, we find, do indeed differ by subject specialty: secondary school teachers leave the profession earlier than do elementary school teachers; and at the secondary level, among teachers of core academic subjects, chemistry and physics teachers have the shortest teaching careers, leaving after only a few years and rarely returning. Chapter 8 outlines principles for more flexible compensation policies that will help the schools to attract and retain teachers whose skills are in high demand elsewhere.

Are we losing the brightest?

Year after year, newspapers lament that our schools are losing the brightest college graduates. Reform reports and education journals make the same point, albeit in less sensational terms: "not enough of the academically able students are being attracted to teaching,"[20] "too many students entering college programs leading to teaching careers are among the lowest achieving graduates of U.S. high schools."[21] How can today's elementary and high school students achieve their full potential if we staff the schools with the least talented college graduates of the previous generation?

Although there was never a golden period in which teaching was the preferred occupation for the nation's brightest college graduates, teaching did offer many advantages for the first twenty-five years after World War II. These advantages included significant autonomy, meaningful work, job security, and an attractive work schedule largely unavailable in other professions.[22] Jobs were plentiful, and there was ample opportunity for mobility. Women and minority group members, particularly, found jobs as teachers during this period, when access to jobs in other professions and sectors of the economy were closed to them.

When school enrollment declined after the early 1970s, opportunities in teaching followed suit. Salaries lagged. Layoffs became common. Students' declining test scores cast doubt on the quality of both America's system of public education and its teachers. After studying the nation's secondary schools in the early 1980s, Ernest Boyer commented that "teachers are deeply troubled, not only about salaries, but also about their loss of status, the bureaucratic pressures, a negative public image, the lack of recognition and rewards."[23]

At the same time opportunities in other professions expanded, and the gains were especially pronounced for women and minority group members. College students responded to the changing labor market, as the historical evidence on the occupational choices of women make clear. In the first years after World War II, 79 percent of Black women who entered the labor market after graduating from college worked in the field of education. In the mid-1980s, by contrast, 23 percent of Black female graduates entering the labor market became teachers. The comparable numbers for White college-educated women are 69 percent for the first years after World War II and 24 percent for the mid-1980s.[24]

The key concern for the future is not simply that teaching has lost its allure, but that it has become particularly unattractive to the brightest and most talented. Academically able college graduates can pick and choose among many career options. If teaching is less appealing to all, it is especially unattractive to those most able to pursue other professions. Why, for example, should a talented biology major become a science teacher instead of a physician? Or a talented history major become a social studies teacher instead of a lawyer? It is a version of Kershaw and McKean's argument once again—for bright college graduates, the costs of becoming a teacher rather than a doctor or lawyer are too great.

In the chapters that follow we examine the ebb and flow of academically talented college graduates into and out of teaching. There is clear and compelling evidence that American schools *are* losing the college graduates who score particularly well on standardized tests. And these students, who have skills valued in many other professions, are lost at every stage of the pipeline: college graduates with high test scores are less likely to become teachers, licensed teachers with high test scores are less likely to take teaching jobs, employed teachers with high test scores are less likely to stay, and former teachers with high test scores are less likely to return.

Losing the "brightest," of course, does not necessarily mean that schools are losing the "best." Because we use standardized test scores extensively throughout our research, we want to be clear about the limitations of such data.[25] There is *some* evidence that *some* dimensions of teachers' cognitive skills are positively associated with *some* aspects of teaching effectiveness. Some researchers, for example, have found that teachers' scores on standardized tests of verbal ability are positively correlated with students' scores and score gains on standardized reading tests.[26]

But individuals who score well on standardized tests are not necessarily better teachers. As Walt Haney, George Madaus, and Amelia Kreitzer document,[27] scores on NTE tests, which are widely used for licensing teachers and which we use in our analyses, are relatively uncorrelated with other, more direct measures of teaching effectiveness, such as supervisor ratings. There are many reasons why this might be so: the tests used to measure teachers' skills may be poor; supervisors' ratings of teachers' effectiveness may be inaccurate; and student scores on standardized tests may be poor indicators of the results of effective teaching.

In fact, this lack of correlation is at the heart of the debate over using standardized tests as part of the teacher licensing process. Although it seems intuitively evident that a solid foundation in basic skills, such as reading and writing, and mastery of the material a teacher teaches should contribute to teaching performance, the research link between test scores and classroom performance is far from established.

The mixed nature of the research evidence leaves us unwilling to interpret teachers' test scores as measures of teaching effectiveness. Instead, we use them as indicators of the quality of opportunities college graduates have in other professional fields. In Chapters 7 and 8, returning to the question of how to measure teaching effectiveness, we discuss the merits of alternative licensing requirements and other strategies to recruit and retain skilled teachers. We argue that basing licensing on applicants' demonstration of their teaching skills is the best way to raise the performance of new entrants to the teaching force.

Why are there fewer and fewer Black teachers?

Between 1965 and 1985, the percentage of minority students in the public schools increased from 20 to 30 percent. At the same time, the percentage of minority teachers declined. This growing disparity between the composition of the student body and the composition of the teaching force is of grave concern. All students in our increasingly heterogeneous society need to be taught by an ethnically and racially diverse set of skilled teachers. They need to see that leadership roles can be carried out effectively by people of different ethnic backgrounds and races.

Almost all data on the career paths of college graduates from minority groups pertain only to Black graduates. Consequently, our research focuses exclusively on Black teachers, as does virtually all prior research on minority group teachers. We study the career choices of Black college students and Black teachers while underscoring the need for recruiting more skilled teachers of all minority groups, particularly Hispanics, into the nation's schools.

In 1970, 15 percent of the students and 8 percent of the teachers in American schools were Black; in 1983, the gap widened to 16 and 7 percent.[28] The declining representation of Black college graduates in the teaching force results from many interrelated factors.[29] One is the increase in opportunities for qualified Black graduates in occupations once closed to them. But ironically much of the problem concerns *lack* of educational opportunity. Because many Black students receive inferior high school preparation, they are less likely than their White peers to enroll in, and graduate from, college. Although such racial differentials diminished somewhat during the 1960s, recent evidence indicates that they are reappearing. Between 1976 and 1988, for example, as the college participation rate for low-income Whites 18 to 24 years of age remained relatively steady (between 37 and 39 percent), the comparable rates for Blacks and Hispanics dropped sharply, declining from 40 to 30 percent among Blacks and from 50 to 35 percent among Hispanics.[30]

States' increasing reliance on standardized tests as part of teacher licensing exacerbates the problem. As we explain in Chapters 2 and 3, most states set their cutoff scores so high that relatively few minority candidates who aspire to teach can obtain licenses. Many Black college students interested in teaching opt out of teacher education programs when faced with the high risk of not being licensed after several years of preparation. If states continue to raise the cutoffs used to license teachers, the situation will worsen even further.

Recent research has enhanced our understanding of why there are fewer Black teachers, but considerable gaps in knowledge remain. In investigating the career paths of Black teachers we ask, as we do for White teachers, how salaries and opportunities in other fields affect their career decisions. Our general finding is that Black and White teachers respond similarly to incentives in and out of teaching. Among both groups, teachers earning lower salaries and teachers with better job opportunities outside of education leave the classroom earlier and are less likely to return.

There are differences in the career paths of the two groups, however. The occupational decisions of Black college students are acutely sensitive to teacher licensing requirements. When licensing requirements tighten, Black college graduates leave the pool of prospective teachers and seek jobs elsewhere. Black teachers are also much more likely than White teachers to start their careers in large urban districts serving high percentages of disadvantaged students. Teaching conditions in these districts are usually very difficult, and both Black and White teachers tend to leave after only a few years on the job. The concentration of Black teachers in districts with difficult working conditions contributes to their declining representation in the teaching force.

This mention of working conditions provides an opportunity to note that this is one subject that we do not examine, despite our belief that working conditions influence the career decisions of teachers.[31] Lacking information on the details of teachers' work environments, we cannot examine how particular characteristics of that environment affect career decisions. As explained in Chapter 5, we do use statistical techniques to verify that our analyses of the impact of salaries on career decisions are not biased by the lack of data on working conditions.

Incentives

In examining any question related to attracting and retaining excellent teachers, the issue of incentives arises. At every stage of their careers, potential teachers, current teachers, and former teachers respond to incentives, and these responses influence who teaches the nation's children. Which incentives work, and which do not?

Chapter 2 describes the decline over the 1970s and early 1980s in the number of college graduates who obtained teaching licenses and examines the influence of changes in licensing requirements on the composition of the pool of newly licensed teachers. Chapter 3 focuses on changes over the last twenty-five years in the characteristics of college graduates who choose to teach, and discusses these differences in the context of new opportunities in teaching and in other fields. Chapter 4 studies the practices school districts use in recruiting and screening applicants for teaching positions. Personnel practices vary widely, and poor practices hamper efforts to upgrade the quality of teaching forces. Chapter 5 examines factors that predict how long teachers stay in the classroom. Teaching salaries and opportunities outside of teaching are powerful predictors of the lengths of teaching careers. Chapter 6 explores factors that affect former teachers' decisions to return to the classroom. On average, one in four former teachers returns, and the likelihood of return depends on the quality of employment options in other fields. Taken together, the evidence presented in Chapters 2 through 6 documents that the career decisions of prospective teachers, current teachers, and former teachers are influenced by the opportunities they face in teaching and in other fields.

In the concluding two chapters we use this evidence to compare the effectiveness of alternative strategies for staffing our schools with racially diverse faculties of skilled teachers, and to argue for the particular strategies we find most promising. Chapter 7 begins with the economic theory of occupational licensing, using this framework to explain why conventional teaching licensing laws are flawed. A system that bases licensing on applicants' demonstrations of their teaching skills, we argue, will attract more talented college graduates into teaching and will also create incentives for improvements in teacher training. Evidence from New Jersey and Connecticut, where changes in licensing laws have influenced who teaches, helps substantiate our recommendations.

In Chapter 8 we draw upon all this evidence to help states and school districts "get the incentives right." We focus first on three popular policies that are often part of efforts to raise standards, but that actually hamper progress toward staffing the schools with more skilled teachers: merit pay, lengthening the period of mandatory teacher training, and requiring that teachers earn master's degrees. In place of these, we offer a set of policies that do promote the goal of raising standards. They include the reform of licensing laws, a carefully structured set of salary increases, and improvements in key working conditions.

An Opportunity for Change

The need to hire two million new teachers in the next ten years is daunting; yet it also provides a tremendous opportunity. Success in designing policies that attract skilled teachers to the nation's schools will affect the composition of the teaching force for years to come—much more so than in the recent past, when relatively few new teachers were hired. The stakes are high. These new teachers will make up the bulk of the teaching force for the first twenty-five years of the next century. If they are primarily academically weak college graduates who could find no more attractive job, the nation will pay the price for many years. If they are among the nation's academically talented graduates, and if they have learned the skills needed to teach effectively, the benefits will be long term indeed.

2

Who Prepares to Teach?

In most industrialized countries, anyone wanting to teach in a public school must obtain a teaching license. As a result, the composition of a nation's teaching force largely depends upon the composition of the pool of people who obtain licenses. In the United States, teaching licenses are granted by individual states, and traditionally, these licenses have been called certificates. But in 1986, the Carnegie Task Force on Teaching as a Profession helped establish a National Board for Professional Teaching Standards, whose mission is to "establish high and rigorous standards for what teachers should know and be able to do, [and] to certify teachers who meet these standards."[1] The current goal of the National Board is not to replace state licensing systems, but to offer "Board Certification" status to experienced teachers who meet the Board's standards. To avoid confusion between the traditional use of the term "teacher certification," and its new use, we employ the term "teaching *licensing* system" to refer to the state-specified requirements that an individual must satisfy in order to teach in a public school in the state.

Although all states require that prospective teachers graduate from a four-year college, specific requirements for teacher licensure vary from state to state. As of 1987, 41 states assess basic skills of applicants, 32 test professional knowledge, 31 test subject content, and 14 require demonstration of competence on the job. Assessment approaches and instruments also vary: 31 states use nationally standardized tests; 16 others use customized tests developed to meet their specific requirements. Even among states that use the same test to assess applicants' skills, requirements differ, because the minimally acceptable score, often called the cutscore, varies from state to state. The most widely used standardized tests are the NTEs. Minimally acceptable NTE scores range from 640 to

649 on the general knowledge subtest, and from 630 to 648 on the professional knowledge subtest.[2] Although this range of cutscores may seem small, even small differences in cutscores can dramatically affect the number of college graduates, especially minority group members, who obtain licenses. North Carolina's proposed increase in the cutscore from 644 to 655 on the NTE Communications Skills Test, for example, is predicted to reduce the percentage of Black candidates who obtain teaching licenses from 36 percent to 5 percent.[3]

The importance of licensure as a gateway into teaching and the variation among the states in licensing requirements raise many questions. Who seeks teaching licenses? Is teaching still an occupation of choice for young women graduating from college, or are young women now choosing other occupations? If young women leave, who takes their place? Does the nature of licensing requirements influence the number and characteristics of new licensees? How do licensing requirements, particularly test score requirements, affect the number of Black college graduates who obtain teaching licenses?

Answers to these questions will allow us to understand better who will be in the teaching force and in the teacher reserve pool in the years ahead. As discussed in Appendix A, it is impossible to answer these questions for the nation as a whole, because no national data exist on trends in the number and characteristics of new licensees. The best we can do is to address these questions for individual states. Here we describe trends in the characteristics of college graduates who obtained teaching licenses in North Carolina from 1975 to 1982. North Carolina is a particularly interesting site for a case study because its requirements for licensure changed in important ways during this period. These alterations allow us to investigate how changes in licensing requirements influence the number of new licensees and the composition of the pool of licensed teachers. Briefly, in North Carolina we find that:

- Between 1975 and 1982, the total number of new teacher licenses awarded each year declined dramatically.

- The decline in the number of new Black licensees was particularly precipitous and reflected, in part, changes in licensing policy.

- The demographic distribution of new licensees changed over time. Younger men and women of both races abandoned the profession, and the proportion of older licensees increased.

- The distribution of subject specialties changed over time, with new licensees abandoning specialties in which jobs were scarce and moving into fields in which positions were relatively plentiful.

We will compare our North Carolina findings with incidental data from other states and with evidence on the training decisions of national samples of college students. These data strongly indicate that the patterns in North Carolina are indicative of patterns in the nation as a whole.

The Shrinking Personnel Pool

Between 1975 and 1982, North Carolina granted teaching licenses for elementary school, special education, or one of ten secondary school academic subjects to 31,956 White and 6,384 Black college graduates who had never taught before in public schools anywhere in the United States.[4] During this period, however, the number of new licenses issued annually declined dramatically—from a high of 6,513 in 1975 to a low of 3,076 in 1982 (see Figure 2.1).

Observers of this precipitous decline might seek explanations rooted in the size of the pool of people *eligible* to seek licenses—the number of new college graduates. In fact, however, between 1977 and 1981, the two closest years for which we have data, the number of students awarded bachelor's degrees from North Carolina colleges and universities *increased* slightly, from 22,804 to 23,143.[5] Thus North Carolina institutions consistently graduated ample numbers of students who were eligible to seek teaching licenses.

The decline in the number of newly licensed teachers was caused by changes in the occupational decisions of college students. For example, the percentage of graduates who majored in education, the specialization typically chosen by those preparing to teach elementary school, declined markedly during this period. In 1977, almost 20 percent of the students who graduated from North Carolina colleges and universities majored in education; by 1981, only 14 percent majored in this field.[6]

The declining interest of North Carolina college students in preparing for a teaching career is mirrored by evidence from the nation as a whole. Figure 2.2, which is based on national probability samples of young women and young men, presents the percentage of college graduates who majored in education, by year of graduation.[7] During the late 1960s and early 1970s, the percentage of graduates majoring in education increased, peaking at 28 percent in 1976; after 1976 this percentage de-

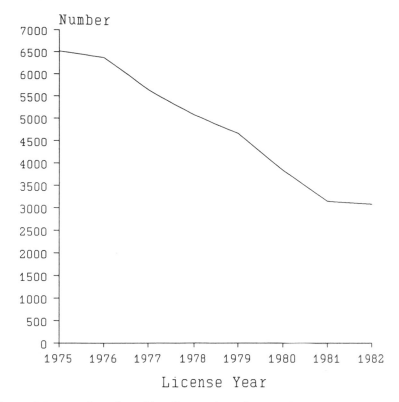

Figure 2.1   Number of teaching licenses issued in North Carolina between
1975 and 1982. (Raw numbers based on the number of licenses
issued in North Carolina to college graduates with no prior teaching experience in another state during the period studied.)

clined precipitously so that by 1984 less than 9 percent of college graduates had a degree in education.

Why did teaching become less attractive during the late 1970s and
early 1980s? The driving forces were demographic and economic. During
the 1970s, after more than two decades of uninterrupted growth, public
school enrollments in the United States began to fall. The "baby boom"
became the "baby bust." Within only a few years, school district personnel officers turned from searching for qualified teachers to staff newly
opened schools to figuring out how to minimize the number of layoffs
due to school closings. Many recent college graduates who had prepared
to teach could not find teaching positions. This sent a powerful message

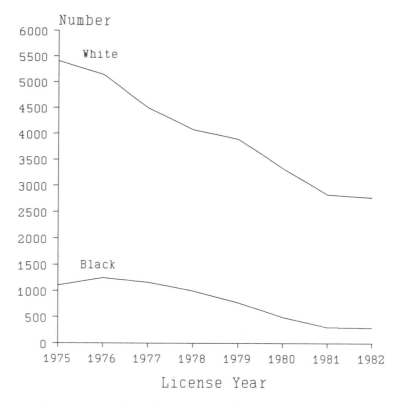

Figure 2.3a   Number of North Carolina teaching licenses by race. (Raw numbers based on the number of licenses issued to Black and White men and women in North Carolina during the period studied.)

period. This was particularly true of Black students, who historically have received relatively low scores on the NTE. We know, for example, that in 1976—the only full year in which the NTE was not required—72 percent of the new Black licensees and 40 percent of the new White licensees did not take the NTE. A similar, but smaller, differential was found in 1975 and 1977, years when the NTE requirement was suspended for only a few months.

Thus part of the reason for the increase before 1978, and the abrupt decline thereafter, in the representation of Black college graduates in the pool of new licensees (Figure 2.3b) is their atypically high representation between 1975 and 1977, the first years for which we have data. Additional data from North Carolina indeed indicate that the representation

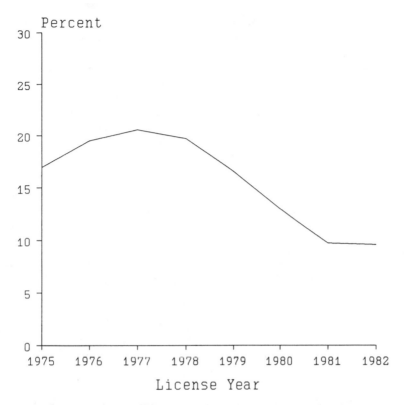

Figure 2.3b   Percentage of licensees who were Black. (Raw percentages based on the number of licenses issued to Black and White men and women in North Carolina during the period studied.)

of Black graduates in the pool of newly licensed teachers was higher in 1976 and 1977 than during the two years immediately preceding.[10]

The temporary suspension of the test-score requirement in North Carolina allows us to evaluate how changes in requirements influence the number of college graduates who obtain teacher licenses. Evidence suggests that the impact of the test requirement was large, particularly among Black graduates. Data from other states support this conclusion. As one recent study prepared for the National Education Association and the Council of Chief State School Officers notes:

> [T]here is clear evidence that disproportionate numbers of minority candidates are being screened from the teaching profession. This exclusionary trend is evident regardless of the state and regardless of the type of

examination—admission or exit; standardized or customized; basic skills, general knowledge, subject area, or professional knowledge. In no state was a trend to the contrary found. Almost without exception state-determined cutoff scores on pencil and paper tests have been set at a level that eliminates a majority of the minority candidates either from teacher education programs or from certification upon graduation, but permits a majority of the white candidates to pass. The nation is moving rapidly toward an overwhelmingly white teaching force.[11]

This trend raises questions about the purposes of test-score requirements for licensure, to be addressed in detail in Chapter 7. Why do states attempt to regulate who can teach in public schools? (There are good reasons, but they are rarely mentioned in debates about teacher licensing.) Are scores on multiple-choice tests like the NTE good predictors of subsequent teaching effectiveness? (They are not.) Would changes in licensing laws increase the supply of skilled teachers, including minority group members, available to the schools? (Changing licensing requirements would make a big difference.)

Gender and age: Most licensees are women, but the age distribution is changing

Women were far more likely than men to seek and obtain teaching licenses in North Carolina. For every year under study, we found that over 80 percent of the new licensees were women, regardless of race.[12] And the proportion of women in the pool of newly licensed teachers remained quite stable; it was 83 percent in 1975 and 82 percent in 1982.

The stereotypic view of the newly licensed teacher is a 22-year-old female college graduate. Figure 2.4a presents trends over time in the age composition of women who obtained teaching licenses; Figure 2.4b presents comparable trends for men. For ease of presentation, we have divided age at licensure into three categories: under 24, 24–30, and over 30 years of age. Given that the vast majority of new licensees were women, Figure 2.4a illustrates that the modal teacher still fits the stereotypic description even as late as 1982. But the pattern is changing.

Most women and men who obtained teaching licenses did so during their twenties. Among both women and men, 85 to 90 percent of those licensed between 1975 and 1982 were age 30 or younger. In fact, the vast majority of new licensees not only were in their twenties but were under 24. This was true for both women and men, but the pattern was

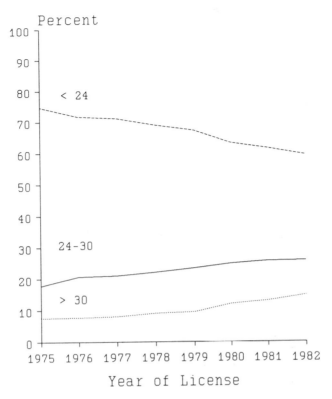

Figure 2.4a Percentage of licensed women in three age groups. (Raw percentages based on the number of licenses issued to women in North Carolina during the period studied.)

particularly pronounced among women; 68 percent of new female licensees were under age 24, compared with 53 percent of new male licensees.

Women and men between 24 and 30 years of age made up the next largest component of the newly licensed pool, with college graduates between 24 and 30 accounting for 39 percent of the new male licensees and 22 percent of the new female licensees. Women and men over 30 represented the smallest component of the pool of newly licensed teachers, accounting for less than 10 percent of all new male and female licensees.

Figures 2.4a and 2.4b allow us to see that the rankings of the three age groups, relative to each other, generally persisted during the eight years under study. The age composition of the pool of newly licensed

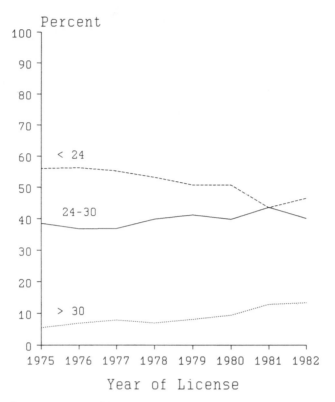

Figure 2.4b   Percentage of licensed men in three age groups. (Raw percentages based on the number of licenses issued to men in North Carolina during the period studied.)

teachers, however, was slowly transformed over time as fewer people in their early twenties obtained licenses and more people in their late twenties and thirties obtained licenses. Among women, the percentage of new licensees who were under 24 declined by about a fifth (from 75 to 59 percent) between 1975 and 1982; among men it dropped by a sixth (from 56 to 47 percent).[13] Conversely, the percentage of new female licensees who were between the ages of 24 and 30 increased by almost one half (from 18 to 26 percent); the percentage of new male licensees who were between age 24 and 30 increased by slightly more than one tenth (from 39 percent in 1975 to 44 percent in 1981) before falling back to its 1975 value.

The most striking age trend illustrated by Figures 2.4a and 2.4b is the *doubling* of the percentage of men and women licensed at age 31 or older.

While the *numbers* of men and women aged 30 and under decreased steadily between 1975 and 1982, the *numbers* of men and women over age 30 remained stable. Given the decreasing size of the pool as a whole, this stability produced large corresponding increases in the percentage of new licensees over 30 and altered the overall age composition of the pool of newly licensed teachers. Among new female licensees, the percentage of women over 30 doubled (from 7.5 to 14.8). Among new male licensees, the percentage increase was even greater, from 5.5 to 13.4. The combined effect of these different age trends is that, between 1975 and 1982, the pool of newly licensed teachers became somewhat "older," with women and men over 30 replacing those in their early twenties.

The aging of the pool of newly licensed teachers is not unique to North Carolina. Data from Connecticut reveal the same pattern. Between 1980 and 1987 the percentage of new licensees who were age 30 or older nearly doubled (from 36 to 60 percent).[14]

Why did the age composition of new licensees change over the late 1970s and early 1980s? One contributing factor is the aging of the general population. Between 1975 and 1987, the percentage of U.S. residents between the ages of 30 and 54 grew from 28.2 to 32.5, while the percentage between 21 and 29 only grew from 15.1 to 17.3.[15]

The graying of the overall population, however, cannot fully explain the changes in the age composition of the pools of new licensees in North Carolina and Connecticut. It appears that teaching lost its allure more for men and women in their twenties than for older college graduates. The decline in job opportunities and salaries in teaching were likely to have their greatest impact on the training decisions of younger college students, who could change career plans at very little cost and without jeopardizing their families' financial security. Meanwhile, perhaps, some of the traditional rewards of teaching—such as shorter structured workdays and vacations that coincide with children's vacations—continued to attract somewhat older people with families.

Different Teaching Specialties for Different Times

School districts do not hire generic teachers, they hire teachers licensed to teach one or more particular subjects. Therefore we must understand not only what happened to the number of college graduates who obtain teaching licenses, but also what happened to the distribution of subject specialties among licensees.

We studied college graduates in North Carolina who received teaching licenses in one of twelve subject specialties: elementary education, special education, English, social studies, mathematics, chemistry/physics, biology, foreign languages, physical education, business education, music, and art. Special education is the field of preparation for teachers who teach children with cognitive, emotional, sensory, or physical handicaps. We treat chemistry and physics as a single field.[16] For ease of presentation, we refer to the last ten subjects as secondary education subjects. Totaling all the teaching licenses awarded between 1975 and 1982 to Black and White men and women, approximately equal numbers were given in elementary education (16,334) and secondary education (17,998). A total of 4,008 licenses were awarded in special education.[17]

The distribution of licensees among subject fields changed over the decade. Although the number of licenses granted in all fields except special education declined, the rate of decline differed by subject. The most noteworthy changes were a dramatic increase in the representation of special education and a decline in the representation of business education. Both of these changes reflect college students' responses to changing job opportunities.

In 1975, 6.9 percent of new teaching licenses were in the field of special education. In 1982, 15.5 percent of new licenses were in this field. This dramatic increase in special education licenses was caused by a change in American education policy, embodied in Congress' passage of Public Law 94-142, the Education for All Handicapped Children Act, in 1975. Public Law 94-142 mandated that, beginning in 1977, all school districts had to identify and provide special education services to all youngsters with educational, developmental, emotional, or physical disabilities.[18] This meant that, while regular education enrollments declined in North Carolina and elsewhere, special education enrollments increased. Between 1976 and 1982, the number of North Carolina children served under PL 94-142 increased by 9.5 percent.

Because these newly identified students needed specially trained teachers, and because a disproportionately large number of special education teachers were needed to fulfill the favorable teacher-student ratios required in special education classes, the number of job opportunities in special education increased dramatically. A growing proportion of students interested in teaching obtained licenses in special education because it was the one teaching field with an increasing number of job opportunities.

Similar logic explains why the percentage of new licensees specializing in business education fell from 3.1 in 1975 to 1.2 in 1982. As we discuss in Chapter 3, business education was also the field in which the smallest percentage of new licensees obtained teaching jobs in North Carolina. Many college students presumably became aware of the poor job prospects in business education and consequently chose other specialties.

Although the shifts into special education and out of business education hold for both Black and White college graduates, the magnitude of the changes suggests that Black students' choices of subject field are particularly sensitive to job opportunities. Between 1975 and 1982, while the percentage of White licensees training in special education doubled from 7.6 to 14.9, the analogous percentages for Black licensees increased more than sixfold, from 3.4 to 21.0. In other words, only one in thirty new Black licensees prepared to teach special education in 1975, but one in five did so in 1982.

The movement away from business education was also more pronounced for Black licensees than for White licensees. Between 1975 and 1982, the percentage of Black licensees preparing to teach business education fell from 9.0 to 3.7, a decline of 59 percent. The corresponding percentage of White licensees fell from 1.9 to 1.0, a decline of only 47 percent.

Not only do many college students compare opportunities in teaching with those in other fields when deciding whether to train to teach; many students also evaluate potential opportunities in alternative teaching specialties. Their actions illustrate a central theme of this book: that the job opportunities and salaries provided to teachers and the costs that individuals face as they prepare to enter or reenter teaching determine who will teach our children.

We do not claim that *all* students, or even a majority of students, pay close attention to opportunities in different fields in deciding whether to prepare to teach, and which teaching field to specialize in. Undoubtedly many students have their hearts set on teaching a particular subject, and they prepare for this career even when job opportunities dwindle and teaching salaries become less competitive with salaries in other fields. We claim only that *sufficient* students, teachers, and former teachers pay attention to opportunities and costs to make the overall pool of people willing to teach responsive to incentives and costs. In Chapters 7 and 8 we discuss the extent to which public policies can influence these opportunities and costs.

3

Who Becomes a Teacher?

Many college graduates who obtain teaching licenses never teach. James Conant, former president of Harvard University, observed this almost thirty years ago when he wrote: "At present it is estimated that only 70% of those prepared for secondary teaching . . . actually take a [teaching] job."[1] At the time Conant made his observation, student enrollments in U.S. elementary and secondary schools were increasing rapidly. There was a teaching job for every qualified college graduate who wanted one. The fact that many of those qualified and prepared to teach chose not to do so is *prima facie* evidence that they found other opportunities more attractive than teaching.

During the 1970s opportunities in teaching declined as student enrollments fell. By the end of the decade, not only were there few job openings in teaching but layoffs were threatening the job security of many incumbent teachers. How did college students respond to these declining opportunities? Did Black college students respond differently than White college students did? Did the most academically able students respond differently than their less academically able peers? What can we learn from the occupational decisions of college students in the past that will help us determine who will teach our children in the future?

This chapter investigates who entered teaching during the years between the late 1960s and the early 1980s. Data from the National Longitudinal Surveys allow us to describe chronological trends in the occupational decisions of college students since the late 1960s. We then continue our case study of North Carolina and ask who, of those who

Michael Schwinden is a coauthor of this chapter.

were licensed to teach, actually became teachers in the state. We find that, between the mid-1960s and the early 1980s:

- There has been an overall decline in the proportion of college graduates who enter teaching and, even among those licensed to teach, a large proportion chose professions other than teaching.

- There has been a disproportionate decline in the number of minority college graduates who become teachers. Changes in teacher licensing policies have affected minority entry into teaching more dramatically than the entry of White college graduates.

- More and more, intellectually able college graduates are selecting professions other than teaching. The proportion of college graduates with high standardized test scores who choose to become teachers has declined dramatically.

National Trends

In the nation as a whole, we estimate that one out of every three students who graduated from college in the late 1960s taught in either a public or a private school within five years of graduation. Over the next fifteen years, however, this proportion declined steadily so that, by the early 1980s, only one in ten new graduates entered teaching (Figure 3.1).

This dramatic decline reflects, to a large extent, college students' responses to the reduced opportunities in teaching that came with declining student enrollments. The number of students attending U.S. elementary and secondary schools peaked at 46 million, in 1971, and declined steadily over the following years to 39 million in 1984. This enrollment decline reduced the demand for new teachers. Those teachers who could find jobs discovered that teaching offered neither the job security that it had in the past nor the opportunity to move, after a few years, to a school closer to home or to a school with more desirable working conditions. Prospective teachers could look forward only to layoffs and to involuntary transfers resulting from school closings.

In the 1990s, job opportunities in teaching will increase again. This will lead to an increase in the proportion of college graduates who prepare to teach, and in the proportion of graduates who eventually become teachers. But who will these teachers be? Will they be the most talented college graduates, or will they be the ones who cannot get good jobs in business and industry? We can make reasonable predictions about the answers to these questions by examining trends in the academic major,

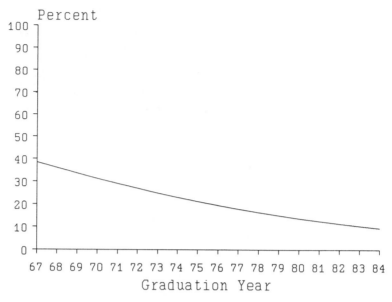

Figure 3.1   Percentage of college graduates who became teachers within five
years of graduation, by graduation year. (Fitted curve, estimated
from Table B.2, Model 3.1.)

gender, race, and standardized test scores of those who became teachers
between the late 1960s and early 1980s.

Race: Minority representation in the nation's teaching force has plummeted

As is illustrated in Figure 3.2, there was a striking change between 1967
and 1984 in the relative percentages of Black and White college graduates
who entered teaching. In the late 1960s, approximately 60 percent of all
Black college graduates entered teaching within five years of graduation.
Less than 40 percent of White graduates made the same decision. During
the 1970s, however, the percentages of Black and White graduates who
entered the teaching profession not only declined but converged. In fact,
in the years after 1981, Black graduates were marginally less likely to
enter teaching than were White graduates.

Two sets of influences underlie the especially rapid decline in the percentage of Black graduates who entered teaching. The first is the increased utilization of standardized tests as part of state licensing require-

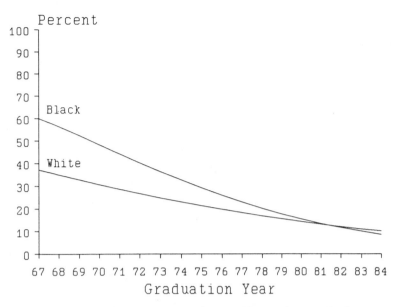

Figure 3.2   Percentage of Black and White college graduates who became teachers within five years of graduation, by graduation year. (Fitted curves, estimated from Table B.2, Model 3.2.)

ments. As discussed in Chapter 2, a greater proportion of Black applicants score below the cutoffs on such tests than do White applicants.[2] Knowledge of this pattern may have led many Black college students to abandon their plans to become teachers.

The second influence is the dramatic increase, over time, in nonteaching occupational opportunities for minority college graduates. Because teaching has been a predominantly female occupation for many years, this trend can be demonstrated most clearly by examining changes in the occupational choices of women. Between 1970 and 1974, only slightly more than one out of every four new female college graduates, regardless of race, worked in professional occupations other than teaching (including accountancy, architecture, medicine, the law, college and university teaching, and the like). Among Black women graduating from college between 1980 and 1984, 62 percent chose to work in these professional occupations (compared with 53 percent of White female graduates).[3] If this trend persists in the 1990s, the nation's teaching force will contain an ever-declining percentage of minority teachers at a time when minority student enrollments are rising dramatically.

Gender: Women are more likely than men to enter teaching

From the late 1960s through the early 1980s, female college graduates were more likely to become teachers than were their male classmates. At least two sets of factors contributed to this gender differential. First, the job of teaching, with a formal work schedule that corresponds roughly to children's school hours, may have been more attractive to women who combined their professional careers with domestic responsibilities as the principal caretaker of their own children. Second, on average, opportunities facing women in fields other than teaching were much less attractive than those facing men during these years. Data from the March 1980 Current Population Survey demonstrate that, in 1979, female college graduates aged 25–34 who were working full time earned 31 percent less, on average, than their male counterparts.[4] Because virtually all school districts in the United States employ uniform salary scales under which a teacher's salary depends on experience and earned degrees, and not on gender, male and female teachers earn approximately the same salaries.[5] Therefore, compared with salaries in other fields, salaries in teaching are more competitive for women than for men.

There was no change between 1967 and 1984 in the relative proportions of male and female graduates who became teachers. Throughout this period, female graduates were 3.5 times more likely to teach within five years of graduation than were male graduates.[6] Thus we expect the gender mix in the nation's teaching force to remain approximately the same in the future as it has been in the recent past.

Academic major: Not all teachers major in education

In our national sample, college students who majored in education were more likely to become teachers than were students who majored in other fields. However, only 53 percent of the students who graduated from college with a major in education between 1967 and 1984 entered teaching within five years of graduation. Over the same period, 15 percent of the college graduates who majored in a field other than education became teachers within five years of graduation.[7] These patterns demonstrate that college major is an imperfect predictor of who will eventually teach. Keeping track of the number and the characteristics of students who major in education provides an inaccurate basis for predicting either the size of the future supply of trained teachers or the characteristics they will have.

Standardized test score: High-scoring graduates do not enter teaching

The National Commission on Excellence in Education, in *A Nation at Risk*, found that "not enough of the academically able students are being attracted to teaching."[8] This finding, which the commission viewed as one factor contributing to the crisis in American education, raises the question of whether the situation has worsened in recent years. Did the teaching profession attract a greater proportion of the nation's most academically talented graduates in the past than it has recently? Using our national data, which include information on IQ, we can address this question for the years between 1967 and 1980.[9]

Throughout this fourteen-year period, college graduates with high IQ scores were consistently less likely to enter teaching than were lower-scoring graduates (Figure 3.3). Moreover, these IQ-related differentials were greater at the end of the time period than at the beginning. In 1967, for example, graduates with IQ scores of 100 and 130 were almost equally as likely to enter teaching. By 1980, however, a graduate with an IQ score of 100 was more than four times as likely to enter teaching

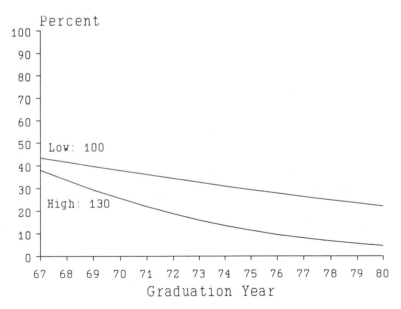

Figure 3.3   Percentage of high-scoring (IQ = 130) and low-scoring (IQ = 100) college graduates who entered teaching, by graduation year. (Fitted curves, estimated from Table B.2, Model 3.5.)

than was a graduate with a score of 130. In other words, by the late 1970s a considerably smaller percentage of new entrants to teaching were drawn from the pool of academically talented college graduates. Furthermore, this was equally true among Black graduates and White graduates, and among women and men.

It is easy to understand why the most academically talented college students were the ones most likely to abandon teaching. When deteriorating opportunities in teaching during the 1970s led college students interested in education to consider other professions, the most academically able found the most attractive alternatives. One reason for this is that high scores on standardized tests are one condition for entry into the graduate training programs for many professions. Students who scored well on IQ tests were also likely to score well on entrance exams for graduate school, law school, medical school, and business school.

We cannot be certain how the occupational decisions of academically able college students will change as job opportunities in teaching improve in the years ahead. But we can conjecture about future trends based on the occupational decisions of a national sample of students who graduated from college during the early 1980s.[10] In this sample, graduates who obtained Armed Forces Qualifying Test (AFQT) scores that were roughly equivalent to an IQ score of 100 were almost twice as likely (9.8 percent versus 5.5 percent) to become teachers as graduates who obtained AFQT scores that were roughly equivalent to an IQ score of 130.[11] Although comparisons of trends across tests must be made cautiously, this evidence suggests that the percentage of new teachers drawn from the upper echelons of the ability distribution was much lower in the 1980s than in the 1960s, but somewhat higher in the 1980s than in the late 1970s. The first comparison is troubling; it illustrates that the schools will need to compete for talented college graduates in the years ahead to a much greater degree than they did thirty years ago. The second comparison suggests that it is not inevitable that teaching will become increasingly unattractive as an occupational alternative for academically talented college graduates.

Salaries: An important determinant of occupational choices

Two questions often arise in discussions about how to staff the nation's schools in the years ahead: Will higher salaries produce a larger pool of teacher candidates? Will higher salaries help the schools attract a larger percentage of the nation's most academically able college graduates? Although our data do not support exploration of these questions, two recent studies shed light on their answers.

The first, by Peter Dolton, shows that the occupational decisions of college graduates in England are extremely sensitive to salaries. The higher teaching salaries are relative to salaries in other fields, the more likely graduates are to choose teaching. This suggests that salary increases in this country will also increase the number of college graduates who choose to teach.[12]

The second study, by Charles Manski, uses information on American college students in the 1970s to explore the role of salaries and test scores in the decision to become a teacher. Manski uses each student's score on the Scholastic Aptitude Test (SAT) as a measure of academic ability. He finds that teaching salaries have a marked effect on the *size* of the pool of college graduates who enter teaching: the higher the salaries, the larger the pool. He also finds that salary increases, by themselves, do not have a marked impact on the *ability distribution* of the set of college graduates who enter teaching. One reason is that graduates with low SAT scores as well as graduates with high SAT scores are attracted to teaching by relatively high salaries. A second reason implicit in Manski's analysis, and a focus of Chapter 4, is that many school districts do not selectively choose the most academically able applicants. Manski infers that the way to increase the average SAT scores of the set of college graduates entering teaching is to increase salaries *and* mandate that all prospective teachers score above a specified level on this test.[13]

Manski did not intend his concluding suggestion to be a serious policy proposal, because he recognizes that SAT scores are not strong predictors of teaching effectiveness. His analysis, however, buttressed by Dolton's, provides two important insights. First, salaries do influence the number of college graduates who choose to teach. Any strategy to increase the number of skilled teachers in the nation's schools must include competitive salaries. Second, to increase the skill distribution of the set of graduates entering teaching, salary increases must be coupled with minimum standards that teachers must satisfy. This insight plays a central role in our discussion of teacher licensing in Chapter 7.

North Carolina Trends

Where does teacher licensure fit into this puzzle? Is licensure a good indicator of the decision to teach, or do many licensees never teach? We turn now to North Carolina and examine whether graduates licensed between 1975 and 1982 actually became public school teachers in the state within three years of licensure.[14]

One caution is needed. Because our data come from the North Carolina Department of Public Instruction, we do not know the occupational status of licensees who left the state. We can only investigate factors that predict which licensees became teachers in North Carolina. This limit restricts generalizations regarding teacher supply at the national level. At the same time, the perspective of the individual state is important. State governments, after all, design teacher licensing requirements with the intent of staffing the state's elementary and secondary schools with skilled teachers.

Details of licensing requirements make a difference

Only 59 percent of the college graduates who were granted a North Carolina teaching license between 1975 and 1982 taught in a North Carolina public school within three years of licensure.[15] This low entry rate is not unique to North Carolina. Wisconsin, for example, has reported that less than half of its recent licensees have become teachers.[16] Just as college major is an important predictor of who will teach so, too, is licensure. Neither the number of education majors nor the size of the licensed pool, however, reliably predicts the prospective supply of teachers.

In North Carolina, the probability of eventually becoming a teacher differed by the licensee's race; however, the direction of the race differential changed during the eight years under study (Figure 3.4). Black college graduates who received teaching licenses during the period 1975–1980 were less likely than their White peers to enter the profession within three years of licensure (51 percent versus 61 percent). Beginning in 1981, the trend reversed; a larger percentage of Black graduates who received licenses in 1981 and 1982 (58 percent) eventually taught in North Carolina than did their White counterparts (54 percent)—a trend that persisted after 1982.[17]

These trends, and their contrast with the national pattern already discussed, are attributable in large part to changes in the North Carolina teacher licensing process. North Carolina has offered two general types of teaching licenses—continuing and provisional. Continuing licenses were awarded to applicants satisfying all state requirements, which included completing mandated academic courses and scoring higher than

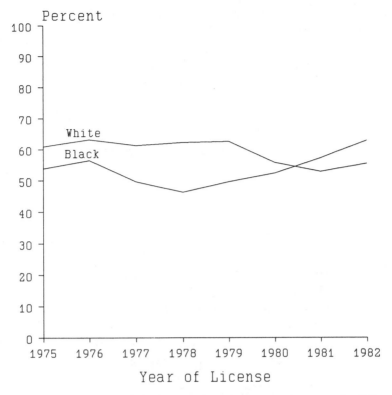

Figure 3.4 Percentages of Black and White licensees who entered public school teaching in North Carolina within three years of licensure. (Raw percentages based on the numbers of Black and White licensees who entered teaching within three years of licensure in North Carolina during the period studied.)

a state-specified cutoff on the Weighted Common Examination Total of the NTE (which we henceforth refer to simply as the NTE).[18] Graduates with continuing licenses could teach indefinitely in the North Carolina public schools. Provisional licenses were awarded to graduates who satisfied some, but not all, of the requirements for a continuing license. Provisional licenses permitted the holder to teach in the North Carolina public schools for only two years, although there was a possibility of renewal if a continuing license was not obtained during this period.

Between 1975 and 1982, licensing requirements in North Carolina changed several times, creating three distinct licensing periods: 1975–1977, 1977–1980, and 1981–1982. The use of applicants' NTE scores in the licensing process, and the frequency with which the two types of licenses were granted, differed quite dramatically among these periods. Although the story we present is unique to North Carolina, it has broad implications because it demonstrates that changes in licensing requirements dramatically affect who obtains a license to teach and who eventually becomes a teacher.

Licensure between 1975 and 1977: suspension of the NTE requirement. Between August 1975 and April 1977, North Carolina suspended its requirement that applicants score above a prespecified cutoff on the NTE. This change allowed many graduates who might not otherwise have sought licensure to be licensed to teach. During these three years, almost one half (46 percent) of new Black licensees, and one quarter (24 percent) of new White licensees, did not take the NTE.[19] Those who did not take the NTE were less likely to become teachers than those who did. Among those licensed in 1976, for example, 47 percent of Black licensees with no NTE score eventually became teachers, as compared with 59 percent of Black licensees with NTE scores. The corresponding proportions for White licensees were similar (47 percent versus 66 percent, respectively).

There are two complementary explanations for this pattern. First, many people who were licensed without taking the NTE were probably taking out "career insurance." They did not intend to apply for a teaching position in the state; for them, teaching was a job of last resort. Second, even among those who wanted to teach, the failure to take the NTE, though legally sanctioned, may have reduced their chances of being hired. Application forms for teaching positions in many North Carolina districts ask for NTE scores. Although scores were not required during the twenty-month suspension period, districts may have been reluctant to make offers to applicants who did not provide scores.

Licensure between 1977 and 1980: reinstatement of the NTE requirement. In 1977, the North Carolina Department of Public Instruction reinstated the NTE requirement. With some exceptions, applicants had to score above a prespecified cutoff in order to receive a *continuing* license. However, between 1977 and 1980, the department granted *provisional* licenses to applicants who did not fulfill all the requirements for a continuing license. Black applicants were particularly likely to be granted provisional licenses, largely because of low NTE scores. During this period, 31 percent of Black and 6 percent of White licensees received provisional licenses.

Provisional licensees of both races were much less likely to teach eventually than were their peers with continuing licenses: 16 percent of the Black provisional licensees, and 19 percent of the White, entered teaching within three years of licensure as compared with 63 percent of the continuing licensees (of both races). The low entry rate into teaching among provisional licensees had a much greater impact on the overall entry rate for Black licensees than for White licensees simply because a much larger percentage of new Black licensees received provisional licenses than did White licensees.

The low entry rate into teaching of provisionally licensed college graduates reflects the decisions of both the school districts and the potential teachers themselves. Districts may have been reluctant to employ provisional licensees because such employment was likely to be time-limited; the provisionally licensed teacher could only remain in the school by upgrading her license. This usually meant that the NTE score must be raised, a risk-laden venture. Similarly, provisionally licensed applicants may have been reluctant to accept teaching positions when offered, because of the very real possibility that they would not be able to keep their jobs. Provisional licensure, offering small hope of long-term employment, was thus little more than a weak consolation prize to the prospective teacher.

Licensure between 1981 and 1982: cancellation of provisional licenses. After 1980, the North Carolina Department of Public Instruction reduced the frequency with which provisional licenses were granted. Instead of being provisionally licensed, most applicants who failed to meet the requirements for a continuing license were denied a license altogether. Between 1981 and 1982, only 6 percent of Black and 2 percent of White applicants were licensed provisionally.

Almost immediately, the number of new Black licensees dropped—a pattern described in Chapter 2. Those Black graduates who received licenses did so by satisfying the same requirements as White graduates, and they received the same type of continuing licenses. And, as we saw in Figure 3.4, the percentage of Black licensees who actually entered teaching in North Carolina within three years of this period is higher than the percentage of White licensees who did so.

Changes in licensing policy led to observable differences between the credentials of many new Black and White licensees. Black licensees between 1975 and 1977 were considerably less likely to have taken the NTE, and Black licensees between 1978 and 1980 were more likely to hold provisional licenses. At least part of the reason new Black licensees were less likely than new White licensees to teach eventually was that school districts paid attention both to the presence or absence of NTE scores and to the type of license that applicants held when employment decisions were made.

Our explanation for the pattern displayed in Figure 3.4 rests on the idea that, in respects that mattered to potential employers, the pool of new Black licensees differed from the pool of new White licensees during the periods 1975–1977 and 1978–1980, but not during the period 1981–1982. One informal test of this explanation is to examine the entry patterns for subsets of Black and White licensees who had taken the NTE and did receive continuing licenses. Entry profiles for these two groups are strikingly similar. Black and White college graduates who took the NTE and received continuing licenses were equally likely to become teachers in North Carolina.

In 1981 and 1982, when Black and White licensees were comparable with respect to having taken the NTE and having received continuing licenses, school districts did not shy away from hiring Black applicants. Indeed, Black applicants licensed in these years were *more likely* to enter teaching than were their White peers, possibly because they were less likely to find desirable jobs outside of teaching.

The lesson of the North Carolina experience is simple: licensing requirements matter. They matter, first of all, because they influence whether college graduates apply for a teaching license. They also matter because the licensing process generates information that employers may consider when they make employment decisions. It follows that the total number of new licensees is an imperfect indicator of the number of college graduates who want to teach, and whom school districts want to employ. Policymakers should use licensure data as a predictor of teacher supply only with great caution and qualification. Second, when examining whether licensing requirements pose an obstacle to the entry of minorities into teaching, not only must the number of minority group members who obtain some kind of license be examined but also the number who obtain qualifications that are desired by employers.

The presence or absence of NTE scores and the type of license were not the only attributes that predicted whether new licensees in North Carolina would ultimately become teachers in the state. We focus next on the graduates who satisfied the most stringent requirements—those who took the NTE and were awarded continuing licenses—and examine how the probability that they entered teaching within three years of licensure was related to their age at licensure, gender, subject specialty, and NTE score.

Age and gender: Women still make up the bulk of the teaching force

Women who were 31 or older when they obtained continuing licenses ("mature women") were the most likely demographic group to enter teaching in the state within three years of being licensed, followed by women under 31 ("younger women"). Male licensees were less likely to enter teaching in North Carolina than female licensees, but again, it was the mature men who were more likely to become teachers than the younger. This ordering holds for both Black and White licensees, throughout the eight years under study.

Table 3.1 presents the percentages of Black and White licensees in each age-gender group who entered teaching within three years of licensure, displayed for the first and last years under examination. Between the 1975 and 1982 licensing years, the probability that younger White women would eventually enter teaching declined dramatically in comparison with the probability of entry for any other demographic group. Younger White women licensed in 1982 were about as likely to teach as were younger White men licensed in that year. Mature women did not desert teaching as rapidly as did the younger women. One possible reason for the age differential may be the extent to which the act of becoming licensed represents a deep-seated interest in teaching as a career. Many women who went to college immediately after high school may have obtained teaching licenses as a low-cost, fallback strategy in case their

Table 3.1   Percentage of Black and White continuing licensees who entered teaching within three years of licensure in North Carolina, by age and gender, displayed for the 1975 and 1982 licensing years.

Age/Gender Category	Black Licensees		White Licensees	
	Licensed in 1975	Licensed in 1982	Licensed in 1975	Licensed in 1982
Mature women	71	63	71	67
Younger women	64	59	70	51
Younger men	62	54	54	49
Mature men	48	40	49	44

Source: Table B.3, Model 3.7.

preferred work in other fields turned out to be unavailable. For women who either entered college for the first time in their late twenties or who returned to school at a later age, seeking a teaching license may have demonstrated a stronger desire to teach than was the case for their younger peers. Combining information about the relatively high probabilities of entry of mature women with the trend described in the last chapter—which shows that the representation of "mature women" in the newly licensed pool is increasing—suggests that fewer and fewer new teachers will be younger women and that more and more will be women over the age of 30.

Subject specialty makes a difference

Teaching specialty is an important predictor of whether licensees will eventually enter teaching. Licensees of both races who trained in special education were the most likely to enter teaching in the state—a consequence of the 1975 passage of the Education for All Handicapped Children Act (PL 94-142), legislation that dramatically increased the demand for special education teachers beginning in the late 1970s. More than three out of four licensees in special education entered teaching within three years of licensure; fewer than one in three licensees in business education did so. These differentials occurred because many college students who were preparing to teach paid careful attention to potential job opportunities when they chose their field of specialization.

Table 3.2 displays, for the first and last licensing years under examination, the percentage of Black and White licensees in each subject specialty who entered teaching within three years of licensure. For both Black and White licensees, the probabilities of entry into teaching within three years of licensure tended to converge over the period studied. The entry probability decreased rapidly in fields in which a large proportion of 1975 licensees became teachers (special education and elementary education), while the entry probability tended to remain stable or even increase in those fields (business education, social studies, and foreign languages) in which a small proportion of 1975 licensees became teachers. This convergence is due to changes in the availability of jobs over time. College students chose to specialize in those fields, such as special education, in which job opportunities became the most plentiful. The ensuing increased competition for jobs among the larger number of licensees in this field meant that a smaller proportion of the available pool were able to enter their chosen teaching career.

Table 3.2 Percentage of Black and White continuing licensees who entered teaching within three years of licensure in North Carolina, by subject specialty, displayed for the 1975 and 1982 licensing years.

Subject-area Specialty	Black Licensees		White Licensees	
	Licensed in 1975	Licensed in 1982	Licensed in 1975	Licensed in 1982
Elementary	80	65	79	56
Special education	77	68	81	67
Mathematics	65	68	67	63
Chemistry/physics[a]			56	54
Art	62	57	53	40
Foreign language	70	76	49	48
English	61	56	60	47
Biology	58	55	67	55
Social studies	54	53	45	37
Physical education	47	43	50	37
Music	41	35	54	40
Business	18	19	32	26

Source: Table B.3, Model 3.8.
[a] There were too few Black licensees in chemistry/physics to estimate these entries accurately.

Throughout the period under study college students responded to changing opportunities in different teaching fields, and the schools were able to find the teachers they needed, such as a growing number of special educators. Can we infer from this evidence that, in the years ahead, college students will provide our schools with the growing number of new teachers of the various specialties that will be needed? College students and other potential teachers will continue to pursue the best job opportunities. Their choices may not necessarily provide the teachers needed in each subject specialty, however, because the 1990s will differ from the 1970s in several crucial respects.

During the late 1970s and early 1980s, job opportunities in teaching were few, and salaries fell relative to many other occupations. The proportion of college graduates training to teach declined precipitously, and those who decided to teach faced an unpromising job market. More and more of these students correctly perceived that, if they wanted to teach, they should become licensed in special education, the one field with rising demand.

During the 1990s, the supply of new workers to the economy will grow very slowly, a consequence of the same "baby bust" that reduced school enrollments during the 1970s and 1980s. College graduates will face attractive job opportunities in many fields other than education. Teaching will attract its share of talented college graduates only if it offers opportunities commensurate with those available in other areas. Those students who do choose to teach are likely to find vacancies in most subject specialties, allowing them to choose the fields they find most attractive. Teaching fields in which the work is particularly demanding are likely to experience chronic shortages, if pay and working conditions are identical to those in other teaching fields. Similarly, fields of specialization that command high salaries in business and industry, such as chemistry and physics, are likely to be areas of shortage unless graduates in these fields are paid a premium for becoming teachers—a proposal we discuss in Chapter 8.

Standardized test scores: Graduates with the highest NTE scores are less likely to teach

Licensees with high NTE scores were less likely to enter teaching in North Carolina within three years of licensure than were licensees with lower scores. Furthermore, a 100-point difference in score had a bigger effect on the probability of entry at the top of the test score range than at the bottom. Thus, although licensees with NTE scores at the 10th percentile of the sample distribution were *3 percent more likely* to enter teaching in North Carolina than were licensees with NTE scores at the median of the score distribution, licensees with NTE scores at the 90th percentile of the score distribution were *8 percent less* likely to enter teaching in the state than were licensees with scores at the median.[20] This pattern, which holds for both Black and White licensees and across all subject specialties, provides further evidence that the most academically able potential teachers are drawn to alternative occupations.[21]

Incentives Matter

The occupational decisions of college graduates are sensitive to incentives. The better the opportunities in teaching, and the higher the salaries in teaching relative to those in other occupations, the more graduates choose to teach. The occupational decisions of the most academically able college students are especially sensitive to incentives. When opportunities in teaching become less attractive, the average academic ability of new entrants to teaching declines.

The evidence from North Carolina also demonstrates that the details of licensing regulations matter. What may initially appear to be relatively minor changes in licensing requirements dramatically affect the number of college graduates, particularly the number of Black graduates, who obtain teaching licenses and become teachers. Those who debate licensing requirements should pay attention to the effects particular changes will have on college students' occupational choices. We return to this theme in Chapter 7.

4

Finding Skilled Teachers: Hiring Practices Make a Difference

Each of the fifteen thousand public school districts in the United States makes its own decisions about how to recruit and screen applicants for teaching positions. Districts also establish their own salary schedules, usually by bargaining with local unions, and they control many of the conditions under which teachers work. Because of local control, some districts are more successful than others in finding, hiring, and retaining skilled teachers. The net result is that the education provided in some school districts is superior to the education provided in other, sometimes neighboring districts, even though the districts appear similar in many respects.

The existence of wide variation in educational quality among school districts in the United States is not a new discovery. In numerous cases litigated in state courts across the country during the last twenty years, plaintiffs have argued that the variation violates state constitutions. The arguments differ in their details, of course, but share a common theme— that many children have been denied equal access to high-quality public education because their families live in districts, especially those with small per student tax bases, that cannot fund high-quality educational programs. In most cases, a simple remedy has been demanded: to change state finance formulas so as to increase expenditures in property-poor districts.

Partly in response to court-initiated changes in school finance systems, per pupil expenditures rose quite dramatically in most school districts over the last fifteen years. Nationally, average per pupil expenditures rose

Joseph Shivers is a coauthor of this chapter.

from $3,088 to $4,348 (expressed in 1988 dollars) between 1975 and 1989.[1] A second reason for the increase was the difficulty many districts experienced in reducing staffing levels when student enrollments fell.[2] A third reason was Public Law 94-142, which added to the student rolls many handicapped students who required expensive services. Although there are many explanations for the expenditure growth, the central point many analysts emphasize is that the increased spending has not been accompanied by discernable improvements in student achievement. In fact, researchers have been unable to find a consistent link between per pupil expenditure levels and student achievement levels.[3]

Education analysts now realize that school districts cannot be treated as "black boxes" that efficiently convert expenditure increases into student achievement gains. Useful policy advice requires opening the "black box," examining school district practices, and learning about what facilitates and what hinders the creation of high-quality educational programs.

In this chapter we examine one part of the black box of school district management—how teachers are hired. Different districts use different recruiting, screening, and hiring processes to fill vacant teaching positions. Certain problems hinder effective recruiting in many districts, but some districts have successfully addressed these issues. We find that:

- In some districts principals and department chairpersons play the key role in recruiting and screening applicants for teaching positions. In other districts, these critical tasks are controlled by the district central office, and building-level supervisors play no role.

- Some districts' attempts to hire skilled teachers are severely hampered by restrictions placed on recruiters. These restrictions sometimes include an inability to offer a binding contract until late summer, to specify the school in which a new teacher will work, or to confirm the subjects and grade the new hire will teach. These restrictions stem both from uncertainty about enrollments and budget and from internal transfer rules that prevent the central administration from knowing, often for months, where a vacancy will be and in which teaching specialty.

- Additional funds, if used creatively, can help school districts to hire effective teachers, even when districts are faced with uncertainty about enrollments.

Hiring New Teachers: Two Case Studies

Until recently, the *processes* school districts use to recruit, screen, and hire potential teachers were ignored by researchers. It was implicitly assumed that competitive salaries and good working conditions were the only prerequisites for attracting skilled teachers to the classroom. Recent studies of school district hiring procedures question this assumption.[4] These investigations suggest that salary increases, by themselves, will not enable some districts to attract better teachers, because inefficient and inappropriate personnel procedures hinder the recruitment of strong candidates for teaching positions. This research also suggests that changes in recruiting and screening practices can help districts to build a strong teaching force.

But before turning to solutions, it is useful to illustrate the extent to which hiring practices differ among districts by describing in some detail the practices used in two northeastern school districts.[5] Although we do not claim that the two districts are representative of any particular population of districts, we do know that the hiring practices of these districts are used by some districts included in case studies commissioned by a National Research Council (NRC) Panel on Teacher Supply and Demand Models.

Grandview, an ethnically and socioeconomically diverse community adjacent to a central city, has a longstanding reputation for providing its residents' children with an excellent education. The district is relatively small, with a total enrollment of approximately 5,000 students; of these, 30 percent are minorities. There is only one high school in the district. The district is widely perceived to be a good place for teachers to teach and children to learn.

Harteville, a large urban community with approximately 20,000 students, and four high schools, provides a poignant contrast. The district has a history of fiscal difficulties. The student population is somewhat segregated, with minority children, who make up approximately 25 percent of enrollment, concentrated in a few schools. Harteville has never been rated highly in terms of SAT scores, per pupil expenditure, or proportion of seniors who go on to college.

Grandview uses aggressive but informal recruiting strategies, relying primarily on networking, personal contacts, and professional organizations. Screening and hiring are almost completely decentralized. The central personnel office weeds out the least promising applicants, and sends a short list of top candidates to school principals. According to the personnel director for eighteen years:

> In a nutshell, our aim is to use the central staff to do a paper screening
> of candidates, to do some initial interviewing, and then to forward as
> quickly as possible as many reasonable candidates as possible to the
> building principal or the department chair [curriculum coordinator] at
> the secondary level . . . and then to let them do the selection. We sort
> of send out a group of people with the Good Housekeeping Seal of
> Approval that are a general batch, and from that general batch the
> principal should choose.[6]

In the high school, the principal delegates the authority to choose among applicants to department chairpersons. The rationale for this practice is that because chairpersons are responsible for the quality of instruction offered in their department, they should be responsible for selecting the teachers who provide that instruction. Chairpersons select a handful of the most promising applicants from the short list and interview them as they see fit, using their own open-ended questions. To obtain assessments of candidates' strengths and weaknesses, chairpersons call references.

Grandview strives for diversity. Chairpersons are not looking for teachers cut from a single mold. An ideal candidate is a well-qualified teacher who brings something unique to the school. The commitment to diversity is not just lip service—during the early 1970s, the 115 new teachers hired by the district came from 87 different graduate backgrounds, 25 states, and 7 countries.

One attribute that chairpersons do seek in applicants is some, but not too much, teaching experience. One chairperson commented that she did not want to hire "a person with a B.A. degree and no experience . . . This is too complicated a school to take children to teach children. If I had my druthers they [great candidates] would have had two years experience in another school so they would have made their really bad [teaching] mistakes somewhere else."[7]

Although the Grandview superintendent is formally responsible for hiring teachers, authority is always delegated to principals, who in turn delegate to chairpersons. Chairpersons need not choose one of the candidates from the short list assembled by the central personnel office. If a chairperson is dissatisfied with all the applicants, the central personnel office finds more applicants. After chairpersons interview candidates, and

for ways to provide timely offers that specify the details of the jobs prospective teachers are being asked to do, including where they will teach and what they will teach.

It is important to understand the reasons many districts use recruiting, screening, and hiring practices that are similar to Harteville's, and the difficulties involved in changing these practices. In some districts centralization and standardization of hiring procedures are responses to perceptions of incompetence or cronyism among school-level administrators. Decentralization of hiring decisions makes sense only if the staffs of individual schools are capable and committed to improving instructional programs.

The internal transfer procedures that create delays in identifying the location of vacancies are benefits for which teachers' unions fought hard. They are perceived by many union leaders as a mechanism to ensure equitable access to positions in the most desirable schools, and as a way of ensuring that teachers who start their careers in difficult schools have something to look forward to.

There are important reasons to alter transfer rules. Not only do they create delays in identifying vacancies, but they also typically result in the most disadvantaged students being taught by the least experienced teachers. These collectively bargained contract clauses cannot simply be abolished by fiat, however. In most states such a move would be illegal; it would also alienate many teachers whose cooperation is critical to improving schools. Changes in transfer rules must be negotiated, and creative solutions found that provide all students with a reasonable proportion of experienced teachers, allow districts to identify vacancies in a timely fashion, and are acceptable to incumbent teachers.

As already noted, the case studies of district hiring procedures commissioned by the NRC Panel on Teacher Supply and Demand Models illustrate that the problems Harteville faces are present in many other school districts, particularly in urban districts serving large numbers of disadvantaged children.[8]

Effective recruiting is commonly hampered by delays in obtaining hiring authorization. Firm offers of teaching positions may not be made until a few weeks before the new school year begins. When early job offers are made, they often do not specify the school's location or the subjects to be taught. This inability to offer firm contracts to strong applicants by late spring frequently hinders districts' attempts to hire skilled teachers. Strong applicants are attracted to school districts that make definite offers.

Delays in providing details of a firm job offer often result from a district's uncertainty about its staffing needs and from budgeting pressures. Because enrollment projections may be inaccurate, staffing needs may remain unknown until late summer or early fall. By law public school districts must serve all children from families living within particular geographic boundaries. In communities experiencing significant in- or out-migration, district administrators may not know until the first day of school how many students will appear, or in what courses they will enroll. During the school year, student migration into and out of specific schools creates additional staffing changes. When budgetary limits sharply constrain teacher-student ratios, teachers often cannot be hired in anticipation of enrollment changes. However, districts with adequate financial resources can offer binding contracts to strong candidates in anticipation of future enrollment increases. This facilitates successful hiring by permitting aggressive recruitment of promising candidates in the colleges and universities during the spring, before less well prepared districts have determined the magnitude and nature of their needs.

Case studies of many school districts document the respects in which internal transfer rules hinder the process of recruiting skilled teachers. The operation of these rules often creates delays of many months in identifying the subject and grade level in which there will be vacancies. In some districts, information about hiring needs is further delayed when teachers intending to resign delay reporting their decisions. In some cases, this occurs at the request of principals who attempt to bypass the internal transfer rules and gain control over who fills the vacancy. By waiting until late summer to announce the vacancy, a principal may be in a better position to argue that the internal transfer rules should be bypassed, and that the vacancy should be filled by a particular candidate he or she has identified. In other cases, teachers delay reporting resignations when contract negotiations are pending because, by being employed on the date when a new contract is signed, they become eligible for improved fringe benefits. The net result can be a wave of resignations during late summer, when qualified applicants are hard to find.

Districts can improve the flow of information about future staffing requirements by negotiating with teacher unions for changes in internal transfer rules. For example, the 1990 contract for teachers in Boston public schools specifies that in schools that have adopted school-based management and have formed a School Site Council that includes teachers, parents, and administrators, the council may choose new teachers for the school without regard to teacher seniority.[9] Other districts have encouraged teachers to announce retirements before the end of the school year by specifying that all retiring teachers will be eligible for any improved fringe benefits negotiated in the next contract.

Adequate funding levels make it considerably easier to renegotiate contract clauses that hamper effective recruitment of new teachers. Districts with adequate funding can offer teachers something in return for accepting changes in transfer rules. In the Boston contract, for example, the changes in transfer rules were accompanied by significant salary increases. Dollars *can* make a difference in facilitating the hiring of skilled teachers. But more money does not *guarantee* more effective hiring practices. Both clear understanding of the problems that hamper recruitment and skilled negotiation to forge creative solutions to these problems are also necessary. Lack of these skills is one reason why the connections between school expenditures and student achievement are so weak.

Adequate funding contributes to the hiring of effective teachers not only by supporting recruitment and screening efforts but also by permitting districts to offer salaries that strong.candidates find attractive. The case studies conducted by the NRC panel revealed large variation in district salary scales. In the twenty-seven districts surveyed, the starting salary for teachers with a bachelor's degree and no teaching experience ranged between $14,420 and $26,061. The salary for teachers with a master's degree and the maximum number of years of teaching experience that the district rewarded ranged from $25,956 to $47,941. Some of the variation, of course, reflects differences in the cost of living in different communities. However, a number of personnel officers from large school districts participating in an NRC conference panel reported that salary played a crucial role in their ability to attract and capture capable applicants.

Some districts with adequate resources attract skilled teachers by providing additional compensation to strong candidates in "shortage fields," defined as subject fields in which there are more openings than there are qualified applicants. Dade County, Florida, for example, includes a $1,000 "signing bonus" (paid in the first paycheck of the second contract year) to new teachers in shortage areas. Shivers reported that Grandview attracts strong candidates in shortage fields by using practice teaching and experience outside of teaching when determining the entering teacher's rung on the salary ladder. Current teacher contracts in Boston, Massachusetts, and Rochester, New York, include specific language that allows similar latitude.

Although we cannot prove that districts' salaries and hiring practices are causally linked to districts' ability to attract strong candidates, personnel directors on an NRC conference panel argued strongly that this was the case. Several assistant superintendents responsible for hiring teachers in large, fiscally stressed urban districts commented that they had lost promising candidates because salaries were not competitive or because they could not make a firm contractual offer when other districts could. The personnel director of one fiscally pressed urban school district commented, "Quality is a luxury that we cannot always adhere to, in staffing the schools."

What will the 1990s bring? We suspect that the role of salaries and hiring practices will become more important as increases in teacher retirements and student enrollments increase the demand for new teachers in most fields. Districts that can offer attractive salaries and better working conditions, that can recruit aggressively, that can screen applicants efficiently, and that can make job offers in a timely fashion are likely to be more successful in attracting skilled teachers than districts that cannot.

What will happen if all districts improve salaries, working conditions, and hiring procedures? Would this result in an upgrading of the average quality of the nation's teachers? The answer depends critically on the extent to which the overall supply of skilled teachers is sensitive to these variables. If the number of skilled teachers is relatively fixed, then salaries, working conditions, and hiring procedures in particular districts influence how this supply is distributed among school districts, but one district's gain is another district's loss. If the number of talented college graduates interested in teaching is very sensitive to the quality of opportunities in the profession, then improvements in salaries, working conditions, and hiring procedures in all districts can improve the quality of education provided to the nation's children.

The evidence that exists on the overall supply of skilled teachers is limited. This stems in part from the lack of reliable measures of teacher quality and in part from the lack of reliable measures of the quality of working conditions and hiring procedures. As reported in Chapters 2 and

3, however, college graduates in North Carolina and in the nation as a whole who prepared to teach during the 1970s and early 1980s were very sensitive to job opportunities, and this was especially true for academically talented graduates. Such data suggest that the overall supply of skilled teachers may be quite sensitive to the salaries, working conditions, and hiring procedures that define opportunities in the profession. Improving salaries, working conditions, and hiring procedures in all districts would do more than alter the distribution of skilled teachers among districts; it would also increase the number of skilled teachers attracted to the nation's schools.

5

How Long Do Teachers Stay in Teaching?

Increasing the number of new entrants into teaching may not stave off a forthcoming teacher shortfall. Shortages of skilled teachers will depend critically on when current teachers leave the classroom. If one tenth of the 2.4 million current teachers leave each year, then 240,000 new teachers must be hired annually to replace them. Even more teachers must be found to staff any new classrooms opened to serve the increasing number of children.

As any school administrator knows, teachers are most likely to leave teaching: at the beginning of their careers, when they first confront the demands of classroom life, and as they near retirement age. This creates a U-shaped "risk" profile for teacher attrition: high in the early years of service, low throughout the middle years, and high at ages near compulsory retirement. In the years ahead the "graying" of the teaching force will further elevate teacher attrition. Over the next fifteen years, the proportion of the nation's teaching force over 55 years of age is expected to increase by half (from 10 to 17 percent).[1] If the replacements for these retirees are beginning teachers, then many of the replacements will probably need replacing themselves within a few years.

How long do new teachers remain on the job? Are career patterns similar in different states? In different districts? Do White teachers remain in the classroom longer than Black teachers? Do science teachers abandon the classroom more readily than teachers of the humanities? Do salaries influence these decisions? We address these questions by systematically examining factors that predict career duration. We find that:

- Teachers are most likely to leave the profession during their early years in the classroom, the first year being the most risky. Teachers who survive the early period are likely to continue to teach for many more years.

- Once the characteristics of the school districts into which they are hired are taken into account, White teachers are more likely to leave than Black teachers.

- On average, secondary school teachers leave earlier than elementary school teachers. Among secondary school disciplines, chemistry and physics teachers are most at risk.

- Teachers with high scores on standardized tests have considerably shorter teaching careers than those with lower scores.

- Teachers who are paid the least leave the most quickly; salary in the first years on the job matters the most.

These findings are based on the career histories of more than fifteen thousand teachers: 6,935 full-time teachers who started their careers in the Michigan public schools between 1972 and 1975,[2] and 9,644 full-time teachers with continuing licenses who took the NTE[3] and who began their careers in the North Carolina public schools between 1974 and 1978.[4] In each state we focus on elementary school teachers and on secondary school teachers of one of six core academic subjects: English, mathematics, biology, chemistry, physics, and social studies.[5] This work is buttressed with information on the career paths of a NLS sample of 612 college graduates who became teachers between 1967 and 1987. The national sample enables us to follow graduates who left teaching into their subsequent careers.

For all teachers in these data sets, we know the duration of their "first teaching spell"—the number of years they taught continuously between the year they were first hired into the teaching profession and the year they left teaching—unless they were still teaching when our period of data collection ended.[6] Forty-four percent of the teachers taught *beyond* the end of data collection, and thus we do not know the full duration of their careers.[7] These "censored" teachers were not ignored in our analyses, however, because the fact that they remained in teaching longer than we were able to observe them tells us much about the potential length of their careers. To incorporate all the teachers in our analyses, we have used a method of statistical analysis known as survival analysis.[8] Rather than focusing directly on career duration—our central interest—we examined the probability that teachers would leave the profession in any particular year, given that they had taught up to that year. We call this conditional probability the "risk of leaving teaching."

The risk of leaving teaching can be estimated just like any other quantity. If many teachers leave the profession during the first year on the job, for instance, then early risks are high. If relatively few of the teachers who remain until their tenth year of service, say, leave during that year, then risk in the tenth year is low. By plotting risk against the number of years of teaching completed, we can create a profile describing the year-to-year changes in the risk of leaving teaching over the entire career.

By comparing risk profiles statistically for different types of teachers, we can determine whether the risk of leaving depends upon the teachers' personal characteristics and working conditions. In this chapter and the next, when we want to illustrate the cumulative effect of differences in risk over longer stretches of the teaching career, we use two summary statistics: (1) *median career duration*—the number of years that pass before half of any given group of teachers leave teaching; and (2) *five-year survival rate*—the percentage of any given group of teachers that we estimate will remain in teaching for more than five years (see Appendix B).

Attrition Is High in the First Years

New teachers who leave the profession do so early in their careers. In Michigan, 21 percent of new teachers left their jobs by the end of the first year, and 13 percent of those who remained left after the second year. In North Carolina, 11 percent of new teachers left after one year, and 8 percent of those who remained left after two years. After this initial "hazardous" period, the risk of leaving declined steadily over time. At the end of the tenth year of teaching, in both Michigan and North Carolina, only about 4 percent of the teachers still on the job left teaching. Figure 5.1 summarizes these trends by plotting the risk of leaving teaching against career length in both Michigan and North Carolina.[9]

Differences between Michigan and North Carolina in the yearly risk of leaving teaching accumulated so that, overall, median first-spell duration in the two states differed markedly. More than half of the Michigan teachers had left the classroom within five years of entry; it took more than eleven years for this to happen in North Carolina. The higher risk of leaving teaching in Michigan probably stemmed in part from teachers

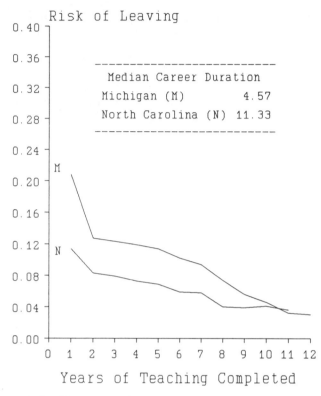

Figure 5.1   Risk of leaving teaching plotted against career length in Michigan (M) and North Carolina (N). (Fitted curves, estimated from Table B.5, Model 5.1, and Table B.6, Model 5.7.)

who quit in anticipation of layoffs caused by student enrollment declines and in part from the weakness of the state's economy, which led many families to migrate to other states.

Over the last fifteen years, the high attrition rate among beginning teachers has hardly affected the attrition rate in teaching as a whole because, during years of declining enrollments, relatively few new teachers are hired. In the years ahead, the schools will hire many more new teachers to replace retiring teachers. The expected high attrition rate among these beginning teachers may increase the overall attrition rate and further raise the demand for teachers. This scenario underlies many analysts' dire predictions of coming teacher shortages.

Two trends in the characteristics of teachers newly hired to replace retiring teachers may ameliorate potential teacher shortages. The first is that many "new hires" are not first-time teachers but teachers returning to the classroom after a career interruption. These teachers have a much lower risk of leaving their jobs after only one or two years than is the case for teachers who are entirely new to the profession. (We discuss returning teachers in detail in Chapter 6.) The second trend is that, as discussed in Chapter 3, an increasing proportion of new entrants into teaching are women over the age of 30 (whom we refer to as "mature women") and this group is generally more likely to remain on the job.

Race Makes a Difference

In Michigan and, to a lesser extent, in North Carolina, Black teachers were concentrated in large urban school districts that disproportionately served poor and minority children.[10] When we compare the 57 Michigan school districts that hired both Black and White beginning teachers between 1972 and 1975 with the 465 Michigan school districts that hired only White beginning teachers during this period, we find dramatic differences: the Black teachers started working in districts that were much larger and contained higher percentages of poor students and minority students (Table 5.1).[11] In North Carolina, the pattern was the same, although each differential was smaller.[12] The Michigan and North Carolina findings parallel those of recent national surveys of teachers. In the nation as a whole, minority teachers are more likely to work in inner-city

Table 5.1 Teacher survival rates in subsets of Mich. and N.C. school districts.

Characteristics	Mich. districts hiring[a]		N.C. districts hiring[b]	
	Both Black and White beginning teachers	Only White beginning teachers	Both Black and White beginning teachers	Only White beginning teachers
Number of districts	57	465	121	20
Average enrollment	51,219	4,784	18,055	4,158
Average % minority	33	1	32	4
Average % poor	23	9	22	18
5-year survival rate (%)				
Black teachers	32		75	
White teachers	30	42	61	66

Source: Last two rows from Table B.5, Models 5.2 and 5.3, and Table B.6, Models 5.8 and 5.9.
a. Between 1972 and 1975.   b. Between 1974 and 1978.

schools, where violence, drugs, teenage pregnancy, and dropouts often present serious obstacles to delivering high-quality education.[13]

Because Black teachers were more likely than their White colleagues to work in large urban districts serving high percentages of poor children, our comparisons of Black and White career patterns take into account the different working conditions that these two groups face. This approach is useful because regardless of race, teachers who work in large urban districts tend to have shorter teaching careers than do teachers working in smaller suburban districts. For example, of White teachers who started their careers in one of Michigan's 57 school districts that also hired beginning Black teachers between 1972 and 1975, only 30 percent were still teaching at the end of five years; of White teachers who started their careers in one of Michigan's 465 districts whose newly hired beginning teachers were all White, 42 percent were still teaching. The corresponding figures in North Carolina are 61 and 66 percent. To account for these differences in working conditions, and the effects that different working conditions have on teacher career paths, our comparisons of Black and White teachers' career paths use a method of statistical control that, in effect, compares the risk of leaving teaching among Black and White teachers *who started their careers in the same school district.*[14]

After controlling for district differences, we find that Black teachers in both states were less likely to leave teaching than were White teachers. Seventy-five percent of Black teachers in North Carolina remained in teaching for at least five years, compared with 61 percent of White teachers who worked in the same districts. Among Michigan teachers, the pattern was similar, though less striking: the comparable five-year survival rates are 32 percent for Black teachers and 30 percent for White teachers.

The career patterns of Black teachers raise two disturbing implications for staffing schools in the future. First, because Black teachers tend to serve in large urban school districts with large proportions of minority group children from low-income families and tend to stay in teaching somewhat longer than White teachers working in the same districts, the declining number of new Black licensees may translate into higher turnover in these districts in the years ahead, as the pool of available new teachers becomes increasingly White. Large urban districts will find themselves on a treadmill, repeatedly hiring new, inexperienced teachers to replace teachers who leave after one or two years. Since the evidence is quite strong that teachers make marked gains in effectiveness during their first years in the classroom,[15] a high turnover rate for beginning teachers can only hinder these districts' efforts to improve the education they provide.

Second, as Black men and women gain greater access to higher-paying occupations, their career patterns should begin to resemble those of their White peers. The earned income of Black college graduates is now approaching that of White college graduates. In 1959, Black male graduates with five years of labor market experience earned 69 percent of the income of White graduates with similar experience levels; the comparable figures for 1969 and 1979 are 85 percent and 88 percent.[16] As opportunities for Black college graduates improve, an increasingly large fraction of those who do enter teaching will be drawn to more financially attractive occupations, unless serious efforts are made to retain them.

Mature Women Stay, Younger Women Leave

In both Michigan and North Carolina, entering teachers who were mature women were the least likely to leave teaching. In Michigan, 64 percent, and in North Carolina, 75 percent of all mature women remained in the classroom longer than five years. Because mature women comprise a growing proportion of all new entrants, turnover rates among new teachers may decrease in the years ahead. This may alleviate the severity of forthcoming teacher shortages.

In both states, "younger" women—those aged 30 or under when they started teaching—were less likely to remain in teaching than were either men or mature women. In Michigan, only about four out of ten of the younger women remained longer than five years; in North Carolina, slightly more than six out of ten remained in teaching for more than five years. We summarize these patterns in Table 5.2, presenting the percentage of teachers who remained in the classroom after five years of teaching in each state. In estimating these percentages we have controlled statistically for differences in subject specialty, and therefore comparisons can be made as though each group were teaching the same subject specialty.[17]

One possible explanation for the short first teaching spells of younger women is that many of them may leave their jobs, perhaps temporarily, to stay at home with their own children. This is consistent with a finding we report in Chapter 6—young women are among the most likely to return to teaching after a career interruption. It is also consistent with

Table 5.2   Percentage of teachers who remained in the classroom longer than five years, by age and gender, controlling for subject specialty.

Age/Gender Category	Percentage of teachers who remained in teaching longer than five years	
	Michigan	North Carolina
Younger women	41	66
Younger men	60	66
Mature men	62	70
Mature women	64	75

Source: Table B.5, Model 5.4, and Table B.6, Model 5.10.

evidence from our national sample, in which almost half of the 283 younger women who left teaching were not in the formal, working-for-pay labor force in the following year. By contrast, *all* of the 104 men who also left teaching were in the labor force in the following year.

A closer look at the national data reveals important changes over the last twenty years in the employment patterns of younger women who leave teaching.[18] One trend is that the more recently a women has entered teaching, the less likely she is to leave the labor force when she leaves the classroom. For example, of the 157 women who began teaching between 1967 and 1974 and subsequently left, 59 percent left the labor force; of the 39 women who began teaching between 1980 and 1986 and subsequently left, only 3 percent left the labor force. This pattern is supported by data from the U.S. Census indicating that the rate of participation in the labor force by women with young children has increased markedly over the last fifteen years.

A second trend in the national data is that an increasing percentage of women who leave teaching to take other jobs obtain employment in professional occupations. For example, 45 percent of the women who entered teaching between 1967 and 1974 and later left for other work outside the home were employed in professional jobs in the year after they left teaching. The corresponding figure for the comparable group of 39 women who entered teaching in the early 1980s is 63 percent.

These trends have two implications for the supply of teachers in the 1990s. First, fewer women will leave teaching to engage in an extended period of full-time childcare than was the case twenty-five years ago. This fact will reduce the attrition rate among current teachers and, consequently, should reduce the demand for new teachers. Second, the so-

called reserve pool of individuals fully qualified to teach, but not currently teaching, will consist of fewer women who are out of the labor
force caring for children full time and more women (and men) working
as professionals in other sectors of the economy. Attracting these members of the reserve pool back into teaching will require salaries and working conditions that are competitive with their current professional jobs,
a topic explored further in Chapter 6.

Elementary School Teachers Stay the Longest, Chemistry and Physics Teachers the Shortest

Accurate statements about teachers' careers must differentiate among
subject specialties. This is true not only because school districts hire
teachers with particular specialties but because, as a result of differences
in opportunities in fields other than teaching, the duration of teachers'
careers differs among college graduates with different fields of specialization. College graduates with degrees in chemistry and physics, for example, as we discussed in Chapter 1, have traditionally commanded higher
salaries in business and industry than have graduates in the humanities.
Consequently, chemistry and physics teachers should be especially likely
to abandon teaching because of the lure of attractive job opportunities
outside of education.

When we investigated the career duration of teachers in different subject specialties, we found striking differences, particularly between elementary and secondary school teachers. Elementary school teachers in
both Michigan and North Carolina were the least likely to leave and thus
had considerably longer first spells than did secondary school teachers
(Table 5.3). In North Carolina, the median first-spell duration for elementary school teachers was more than 11 years, and in Michigan it was
almost 6 years. Among secondary school teachers, average career duration ranged from a minimum of just over 2 years to a maximum of 4.5
years in Michigan and from a minimum of 5.6 years to a maximum of
more than 11 years in North Carolina, depending on the subject specialty.[19]

Chemistry and physics teachers were most likely to leave teaching in
each of the first 10 years, leading to the very short median first spells
displayed in Table 5.3. In Michigan, almost half the chemistry and physics teachers had left teaching by the end of 2 years in the classroom; in
North Carolina, more than half had left within 6 years.

Table 5.3   Median teaching career duration (in years) by subject specialty, controlling for age, gender, and race.

Subject Specialty	Michigan	North Carolina
Elementary	5.9	> 11.0
Secondary	3.9	7.8
Biology	4.5	5.9
Social studies	4.0	8.8
English	3.7	6.4
Mathematics	3.6	> 11.0
Chemistry/physics	2.2	5.6

Source: Table B.5, Models 5.4 and 5.5, and Table B.6, Models 5.10 and 5.11.

By contrast, mathematics teachers had a median first spell more than 1 year longer than that of chemistry and physics teachers in Michigan and over 5 years longer in North Carolina. These differentials are surprising because, as Figure 1.1 illustrates, college graduates trained in mathematics who entered business and industry earn approximately the same starting salaries as college graduates trained in physics and chemistry.

One possible explanation for this discrepancy is that many secondary-school mathematics teachers do not have the technical skills demanded by business and industry. Had we been able to distinguish mathematics teachers prepared to teach calculus and computer programming from those prepared to teach basic math and introductory algebra, perhaps we would have observed career patterns corresponding more closely to our hypothesis. In Chapter 6 we report that mathematics teachers who do leave teaching have a particularly low probability of returning. This supports our conjecture that it is the subset of mathematics teachers who are able to get good jobs in business and industry that are most likely to leave the classroom.

A recent report from the Connecticut State Department of Education supports the conjecture that the undergraduate preparation of many mathematics teachers limits their options outside of teaching, and helps explain why they stay in teaching longer than do chemistry and physics teachers. Less than half the teachers newly hired in 1988 to teach mathematics in Connecticut had an undergraduate major in mathematics or in one of the sciences. Thus more than half of the newly hired mathematics teachers lacked the credentials necessary to obtain high-paying positions in business and industry. In contrast, more than 90 percent of the teachers newly hired to teach the physical sciences had undergraduate majors in either physical or life science.[20]

The combined evidence from both Michigan and North Carolina suggests that although short first spells contributed to a shortage of chemistry and physics teachers, the same was not true for mathematics teachers. If there is a shortage of mathematics teachers, it stems from either a smaller number of college-trained mathematicians entering teaching or a lower proportion of mathematics teachers returning to the classroom after a career interruption, a possibility we explore in Chapter 6.

Finally, in Michigan chemistry/physics teachers and biology teachers differed considerably in their career duration, with biology teachers staying more than two years longer. (The differential in North Carolina is much smaller, but in the same direction.) The Michigan pattern suggests that, at least in terms of career duration, biology and chemistry/physics teachers should not be grouped together under the rubric "science" teachers. The discrepancy in career duration between the sciences also adds weight to our contention that attractive alternative opportunities pull many teachers from the classroom. Biology majors who have taken positions in business and industry have earned considerably less than their peers who majored in chemistry and physics (see Figure 1.1).

Teachers with High Test Scores Leave

We found that first-spell duration was strongly related to scores on the NTE for teachers in North Carolina. (No test-score data are available for Michigan teachers.) Teachers with high NTE scores were less likely to remain in the classroom than those with lower scores, and this differential held for both experienced and beginning teachers. Even among teachers with ten years of experience, those with high scores were more likely to leave teaching than those with low scores. This compelling pattern of differentials in career duration corroborates our hypothesis that many teachers' career choices are influenced by incentives, because high-scoring teachers have greater access to high-paying occupations than do teachers with lower scores.[21]

Table 5.4 displays the estimated percentage of teachers whose first spells were longer than five years, for prototypical teachers at the median, the 10th percentile, and the 90th percentile of the sample distribution, among both Black and White college graduates. Note that small differences in test scores among high-scoring teachers corresponded to larger

Table 5.4   Percentage of Black and White teachers remaining in teaching longer than five years in North Carolina, by NTE score, controlling for age, gender, and subject specialty.

| Race | NTE score | | Percentage of teachers remaining in teaching longer than five years |
	Percentile	Score	
Black	90	584	74
	50	490	78
	10	432	80
White	90	700	56
	50	600	65
	10	503	71

Source: Table B.6, Model 5.12.

differences in career duration than similar differences in scores among low-scoring teachers.[22] This pattern is especially important for understanding the relationship between test score and the risk of leaving teaching among Black teachers. In the data presented in Table 5.4, NTE score seems to matter less among Black teachers. This is not because the relationship between NTE score and the risk of leaving teaching differed by race. Rather, the differences among the five-year survival percentages were smaller because nine out of ten Black teachers had NTE scores that were lower than the median score among White teachers. Black teachers' NTE scores fell in the range in which large score differences had a smaller impact on the risk of leaving teaching. Among the relatively few Black teachers with high NTE scores, a 100-point score differential was associated with just as large a difference in career duration as was the case for White teachers. This suggests that, if the test scores of Black teachers continue to increase through improved educational opportunity in the future, the career patterns of more Black teachers will begin to resemble those of high-scoring White teachers.

We also find this "highest-scoring/earliest-leaving" pattern in the national sample. Teachers with high IQ scores were more likely to leave teaching at the end of each year of service than those with low scores. These risk differentials resulted in a median career duration for teachers with IQ scores at the 90th percentile of the sample distribution that was more than 1.7 years shorter than the median career duration for teachers with IQ scores at the 10th percentile.[23]

In considering the implications of these test-score findings, it is instructive to compare the experiences of private schools and public schools. Other research suggests that private schools have been more successful than public schools in recruiting teachers with very high scores on the Scholastic Aptitude Test. Yet high-scoring teachers in private schools have been more likely than their high-scoring peers in public schools to leave after only a short spell in the classroom.[24] This public–private comparison suggests that, if the public sector wants to increase the number of academically talented college graduates in its schools, an effective strategy may be to make entry into teaching easier for these graduates, while accepting that many of them may resign after a few years to pursue other careers. We discuss this issue in more detail in Chapter 7.

Teachers Who Are Paid More Stay Longer

In both Michigan and North Carolina, teachers working in school districts offering comparatively high salaries stayed longer than teachers working in districts offering low salaries.[25] To illustrate this pattern, we plot, in Figure 5.2a, the risk of leaving teaching for three prototypical secondary school teachers in Michigan: one in an average salary stream, one in a low salary stream ($2,000 less per year than average, in 1988 dollars), and one in a high salary stream ($2,000 more per year than average, in 1988 dollars).[26] Although our analyses incorporate data from all the Michigan teachers described at the beginning of this chapter, we display our findings only for those teachers who were hired in 1972. As we explain below, the impact of salary on first-spell length is smaller for teachers who entered teaching in Michigan schools in the later years. Figure 5.2b displays equivalent risk profiles for comparable teachers newly hired by North Carolina school districts.

Teachers with relatively low salaries were more likely to leave teaching than were better-paid teachers. Moreover, salary had its greatest impact on the risk of leaving during the first years on the job. A teacher in the below-average salary stream was approximately one and a half times more likely to leave at the end of the first year than a teacher in the above-average salary stream. These large salary-related differences in risk during the early years of teaching accumulate and result in large differences in median first-spell length among teachers paid at different levels. For secondary school teachers in Michigan, an annual salary differential of $2,000 was associated with a difference in median employment dura-

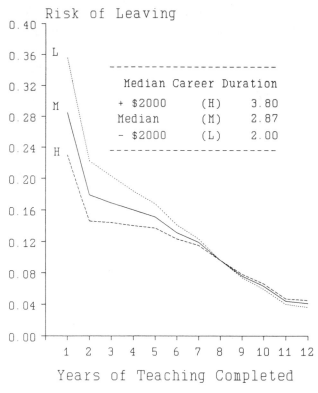

Figure 5.2a   Risk of leaving teaching for entering secondary school teachers in high, median, and low salary streams in Michigan. (Fitted curves, estimated from Table B.5, Model 5.6.)

tion of approximately one year; in North Carolina the differential was almost two years.[27]

Salaries were also associated with the duration of first spell for elementary school teachers, although the size of the effect was somewhat smaller, particularly in Michigan.[28] Table 5.5 presents the percentage of elementary and secondary school teachers remaining in the classroom beyond five years in high, median, and low salary streams. The effect of salary was most pronounced among beginning elementary school teachers and diminished steadily as teachers gained experience—as was the case among secondary school teachers.[29] And, like secondary school teachers, highly paid elementary school teachers tended to remain in teaching considerably longer than those who were paid less.

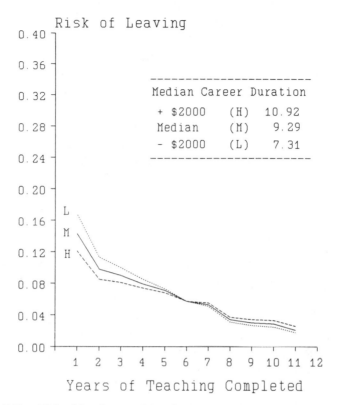

Figure 5.2b Risk of leaving teaching for entering secondary school teachers in high, median, and low salary streams in North Carolina. (Fitted curves, estimated from Table B.6, Model 5.13.)

Table 5.5 Percentage of elementary and high school teachers who stayed in teaching longer than five years, by salary, controlling for age, gender, subject specialty, entry cohort, race, and district characteristics (and NTE score in North Carolina).

Salary Stream	Michigan		North Carolina	
	Elementary	Secondary	Elementary	Secondary
$2,000 above median	54	42	79	64
Median	49	35	77	60
$2,000 below median	43	27	74	56

Source: Table B.5, Model 5.6, and Table B.6, Model 5.13.

The strength of the salary effect declined over time so that by the eighth year of a teaching career in Michigan and the sixth year in North Carolina, salary had no differential effect at all. Two complementary factors may explain the declining impact of salary. First, switching to a new occupation becomes less attractive as teachers gain experience. They acquire skills, such as the ability to handle discipline problems, that make teaching more pleasant, and they develop networks of friends and colleagues. Occupational alternatives become more limited as they age, because many firms want to hire only recent college graduates. Second, among all teachers (and perhaps especially among those in relatively low-paying districts), those whose career choices are most sensitive to salary depart early, leaving those teachers whose career choices are relatively insensitive to salary inducements.[30]

In interpreting our salary results, we were concerned about two possible sources of bias, both stemming from differences in working conditions among districts. On the one hand, districts paying high salaries often offer desirable working conditions that themselves are responsible for longer teaching careers. Overlooking these influences might lead to *overestimation* of the potential effect that salary has on career duration. On the other hand, some districts with difficult working conditions offer higher salaries as compensation for the adverse conditions that might lead to resignation after a short spell of teaching. Overlooking these influences might result in *underestimation* of the potential effect of salary on career duration.

We adopted two strategies to take into account the influences of working conditions. First, in the findings reported so far in this section, school district characteristics are controlled by including them as predictors in our analyses. The included characteristics were: (1) the median household income of families residing in the school district, (2) the median level of the adult population's education, (3) the proportion of children under 18 who live below the poverty level, (4) the proportion of adults who work in professional occupations, and (5) the proportion of the population that is Black or Hispanic.[31] These variables provided information on the characteristics of the families living in each school district and served as proxies for unobserved variables that might have influenced career duration.

We then repeated our analyses using the "fixed-effects" method of statistical control, in order to examine salary and career duration as though all teachers were employed in the same school district.[32] Such a "district-specific" strategy disentangles the influence of salary on duration from the influences of all other district characteristics that do not vary over time, allowing reexamination of our initial findings controlling for the influence of school district characteristics. Our district-specific analyses yielded virtually identical results in North Carolina and stronger results in Michigan.[33] These patterns give us confidence that our findings do not overestimate the impact of salary on length of stay in teaching.[34]

Finally, as already mentioned, the salary effects detected in Michigan are larger for teachers hired in 1972 than for teachers hired in the subsequent three years. We believe this difference is due to declining student enrollments. Between 1972 and 1975, enrollments in Michigan declined by 3 percent, and it was evident that the decline would continue. As enrollment declines reduced the demand for teachers, the impact of salary on career decisions may have been dwarfed by concerns about the lack of opportunity for desirable transfers, or even about possible layoffs.

In North Carolina, the association between salary and career duration was similar across all five of our entering cohorts, from 1974 through 1978. We expected such similarities, because student enrollments were stable in these years in North Carolina. Student enrollments did decline in North Carolina by 5 percent, however, between 1979 and 1982. When we analyzed data on teachers who began to teach in North Carolina during those years, we found no relationship between salary and the risk of leaving teaching. We conclude that teacher career decisions are more affected by salaries during the years when demand for teachers is stable or growing than in periods when demand is declining. During the 1990s, when demand for new teachers will grow once again, salaries will again come to play a crucial role in determining how long teachers remain in the classroom.

Staffing the Schools in the 1990s

The number of teachers leaving the classroom will increase during the 1990s as the large number of teachers hired during the 1950s and 1960s reach retirement age. Whether the nation succeeds in providing all children with qualified replacements will depend critically on the length of time new entrants remain the classroom. In this chapter, we have showed that beginning teachers working in Michigan schools were much more likely to leave teaching than were teachers with the same amount of experience working in North Carolina schools. This reflects profound differences between the economies and demographics of the two states. Yet despite these differences between the states, salary and the quality of alternative opportunities outside of teaching were related to length of stay in teaching for teachers in both states. Teachers who were paid more were more likely to stay longer in teaching. Teachers whose specialties and test scores gave them the best occupational alternatives were the most likely to leave teaching. These findings illustrate the importance of economic factors, both within teaching, and in alternative occupations, in determining how long new teachers stay in the profession. In Chapter 8, we describe policies that hold promise for inducing talented college graduates to stay in teaching long enough to be of real service.

6

Who Returns to Teaching?

Conventional wisdom assumes, as do most published reports on teacher career mobility, that teachers who leave the classroom never return. In a recent article describing the experiences of four women who left teaching to pursue other careers, Beverly Kempton writes: "Each of these four women abandoned the teaching profession to embark on a career alien to her background. They moved on, but they did not abandon their former selves. Over time, their teaching skills evolved into management skills, forming the bedrock of a new career. The risks were great, but the rewards even greater: excitement, money, challenges, opportunities."[1] The myth that teacher mobility occurs in only one direction drives most current models of teacher supply and demand, and newly minted college graduates are thus seen as the only source of teacher supply.

Yet recent research on teacher supply demonstrates that many former teachers do return to the classroom. Kay Scheidler, who quit teaching high school English to work in computer sales and subsequently returned to the classroom, describes why she left teaching:

> Teachers . . . have a set of beliefs that we regularly reinforce with each other. We believe that every other profession offers greater independence, higher pay, more respect, and better working conditions. Other professionals enjoy leisurely lunch breaks and can leave their work behind them at 5:00. Above all, we believe, the quality of their days is different because they don't have to face 120 adolescents for 6 hours each day. For women in education, these myths can raise an added doubt. Are we trapped in a low-status, traditional nurturing profession while all the smart, well educated, competitive women are in respected fields that reward their successes?[2]

And why she returned:

> I knew I could sell successfully; I also knew I didn't want to. My hesitation was over: give me back Shakespeare, Ibsen, even Hinton and Zindel. I saw many, many smart, talented people working for less money, longer hours, under worse conditions than I'd had as a teacher. The myths were shattered. The rest of the world wasn't so glamorous and rewarding after all. Give me back my ninth graders, my summers, bungling administrators, my teacher friends, the constant debate of what's right and wrong, my own classroom and desk. You can't escape ninth graders anyway, I decided. They're everywhere.[3]

Our research convinces us that Kay Scheidler's story is common. There may be, in fact, enough returnees to fill many of the teacher vacancies expected in the years ahead. State and national surveys of the backgrounds of newly hired teachers show that, in the late 1980s, many newly hired teachers came from the "reserve pool"—a term used to describe those either returning to teaching after a career interruption or licensed a number of years earlier and now entering the teaching force for the first time. The Connecticut State Department of Education, for example, reports that three quarters of all teachers newly hired in 1986 were members of the reserve pool.[4] In New York State, almost the same proportion (70 percent) of new hires were drawn from the same source.[5]

That the reserve pool is an important source of teacher supply is not a new insight. James Conant, writing in the early 1960s, pointed out that "a considerable number of former teachers or those prepared some years ago enter the classroom each year."[6] Surveys in the mid-1980s by the National Education Association (NEA) indicate that the reserve pool is becoming an increasingly important source of teacher supply. In 1986 more than eight out of every ten teachers newly hired into the nation's public schools were members of the reserve pool; in 1966 reserve pool members represented only three out of every ten new hires.[7]

The increasing importance of the reserve pool as a source of teacher supply raises new questions for the 1990s. How large is the reserve pool? Among teachers entering the reserve pool, what percentage will return to teaching and how long, on average, will they wait before doing so? Are women more likely to return than men? Are all subject specialties adequately represented in the reserve pool, and are teachers of some subjects more likely to return than others?

We investigated the career behavior of North Carolina and Michigan teachers who ended a first teaching spell prior to the final two years of observation, and who were therefore able to return to teaching during the period covered by our study. To answer our questions, we examined the roles that demographic characteristics and measures of opportunity cost played in predicting how long teachers spent away from teaching before returning to the classroom (if they ever returned).[8] Our analytic strategy was very similar to that used earlier to examine the length of the first teaching spell; in this case, however, we sought factors associated with the "risk" of a *return to teaching* after a first teaching spell had ended. To avoid the negative connotation of the term "risk," we use the term "rate of reentry" to refer to the probability that a teacher ends a career interruption in any particular year to reenter teaching, given that he or she has been out of the classroom up to that year.

Our samples contained 4,283 teachers from North Carolina 4,676 teachers from Michigan, and 456 teachers from the NLS. Our state databases contain no information on the occupational experiences of former teachers. This information is available, however, for the teachers in our national sample who left the classroom. We use the national data to explore whether former teachers' decisions to reenter teaching are related to the type of work they did after they left teaching.[9] Because we detected no differences between the reentry behaviors of Black and White teachers, we report combined results for these groups. Briefly, we found that:

- Approximately one out of every four teachers who left teaching eventually reentered the profession. Most career interruptions were short; one year was the most common length of time that a teacher remained out of the classroom.

- Women who were 30 years or older at the time they left teaching were more likely to return than either younger women, or men of any age. Men who were under 30 years of age when they left teaching were the least likely to return.

- Elementary school teachers were more likely to reenter teaching after a career interruption than were secondary school teachers. Among secondary school teachers, former chemistry and physics teachers were less likely to return than former teachers of other core academic subjects.

- Former teachers with high scores on the NTE were especially unlikely to return to teaching.

Most Career Interruptions Are Short

The longer a teacher is away from the classroom, the less likely he or she is to return. This pattern, found in both Michigan and North Carolina, is illustrated in Figure 6.1, which presents the rate of reentry plotted against the length of time teachers have been out of the classroom for the two state samples. This overall pattern is, of course, not surprising. Teachers who leave their jobs for only one year are likely to have taken a leave of absence to care for children, to return to school, or to cope with illness. Many intend to return to the classroom, and do so as quickly as they can. Those who spend three or more years away from the classroom, by contrast, probably find work in other fields and do not intend

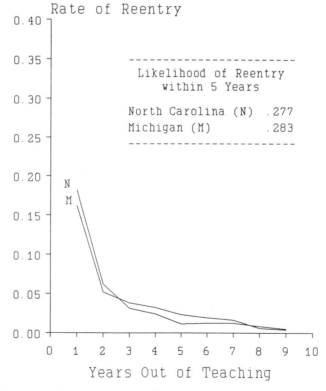

Figure 6.1 Rate of reentry into teaching after termination of a first spell plotted against the length of time teachers have been out of the classroom in Michigan (M) and North Carolina (N). (Fitted curves, estimated from Table B.9, Model 6.1 and Table B.10, Model 6.4.)

to reenter teaching—although as Kay Scheidler indicates, some change their minds.

Our findings in North Carolina and Michigan are remarkably similar. Of teachers from both states who left teaching, one in six returned after one year. Of those who stayed out for a second year, one in twenty returned. The longer a teacher stayed away, the smaller were the chances of reentry. Despite the rapidly declining rate of reentry, the cumulative probability that teachers who left the classroom would eventually return was quite high. In both states, 28 percent of teachers who left teaching during our period of observation returned within five years. Among teachers in our national sample, whom we were able to follow across state lines, we found the same pattern—28 percent of teachers who left the classroom returned within five years. Of those remaining, an additional one out of every eight returned to the classroom after interruptions ranging from six to twelve years.[10] The extraordinary consonance in the evidence from the two state samples and the national sample demonstrates conclusively that newly minted college graduates are not the only source of new hires; teachers returning to the classroom after career interruptions are an extremely important source of supply.

Women Are More Likely to Return than Men

Among teachers from both states who left teaching, women were more likely to return than men. Almost one in three women, as compared with one in five men, returned to the classroom within five years of a career interruption. The conventional explanation for this pattern is that many women who leave teaching do so to stay at home with their children. When these women are ready to reenter the labor force, they return to the classroom in part because teaching provides a work schedule particularly compatible with their childcare needs.[11]

Our national sample provided information on the occupational status of former teachers and permitted us to explore the validity of this explanation. We found that 57 percent of the female teachers who left teaching during the period 1970–1979 were out of the labor force in the subsequent year. Of this group, 47 percent returned to teaching within five years. Thus, at least in the 1970s, conventional wisdom seems to be supported. But women's employment patterns are changing. Only 30 percent of the women who left teaching during the 1980s were out of the labor force in the subsequent year and, of these, only 36 percent returned to teaching within five years. Over time, a declining proportion of the reserve pool will consist of women out of the labor force.

Do former teachers who take positions in other sectors of the economy eventually return to teaching? The evidence from our national sample suggests that the pattern differs both by gender and by the new occupational status of the former teachers, and that it is changing over time. Figure 6.2 presents a profile of the percentage of teachers who reenter teaching within five years of leaving the classroom, displayed by exit year, by gender and by whether the teachers worked in a professional occupation after they left teaching.

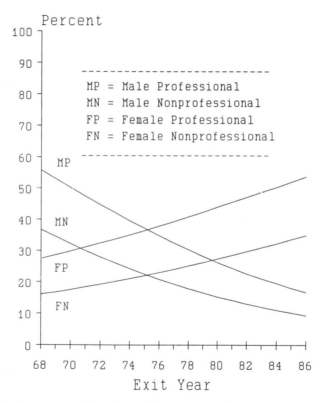

Figure 6.2 Percentage of teachers who reenter teaching within five years of ending a first spell plotted against year of original exit from the profession, by gender and by whether the teachers worked in a professional occupation after leaving the classroom. (Fitted curves, estimated from Table B.11, Model 6.8.)

One surprise was the finding that women and men who took jobs in professional occupations after leaving teaching were more likely to return to the classroom than were individuals who took jobs in nonprofessional occupations. We predicted the opposite pattern, based on the assumption that jobs in professional occupations were more attractive than jobs in nonprofessional occupations. One explanation for the observed pattern is that our assumption may not be true. A second is that individuals who took jobs in professional occupations may have found it easier to find another teaching position than did individuals working in nonprofessional occupations. Since the trend over time in the likelihood of a return to teaching is the same for women and for men who worked in either professional or nonprofessional occupations, we focus on individuals in professional occupations in describing the other patterns displayed in Figure 6.2.

Among women who left teaching for professional jobs, those who left in the 1980s were more likely to return than those who left in the 1970s. Approximately one in three women who left teaching in the early 1970s to pursue other professional employment reentered teaching within five years; one in two who left during the early 1980s returned to the classroom within five years. This pattern suggests that Kay Scheidler's experience may mirror that of other women who leave teaching only to return eventually, and that this group is growing.

In contrast, the percentage of men who reenter teaching after pursuing work in other sectors is declining. Approximately one in two men who left teaching in the early 1970s for other professional employment returned within five years; only one in five who left in the early 1980s returned within five years. Discrimination in labor markets outside of education may explain this gender differential. During the 1970s, employment opportunities for women in fields outside of teaching improved, allowing more and more women to take positions in other fields. But wage differentials between men and women in these fields remained. In 1979, for example, female college graduates aged between 25 and 34 who were working full time earned 31 percent less than their male peers.[12] Wage inequity may have persuaded many women to reconsider teaching, a field in which salaries depend solely on experience and earned degrees.

In the years ahead, fewer teachers who leave the classroom will leave the labor force. A declining proportion of teaching vacancies will thus be filled by women returning to teaching after a period out of the labor force. Not all who leave teaching for work in other sectors of the economy find it more rewarding. Many, especially women, do not, and return to teaching.[13]

Elementary Teachers Are the Most Likely to Return, Chemistry and Physics Teachers the Least Likely

In both North Carolina and Michigan, elementary school teachers were more likely to reenter teaching after a career interruption than were secondary school teachers (see Table 6.1). The best explanation for this phenomenon is the one we proposed in Chapter 5 for the relatively long first teaching spells of elementary school teachers—namely, that alternative employment opportunities available to elementary school teachers are less attractive than those typically available to (secondary school) teachers who possess a specific disciplinary specialty.[14]

Among secondary school teachers, the cumulative five-year probability of a reentry into teaching differed among the subject specialties. In both states, chemistry and physics teachers were much less likely to return to the classroom within five years than teachers of other subjects. The low rate of reentry among chemistry and physics teachers—only one in six was predicted to return within five years—supports the hypothesis that teachers' career decisions are sensitive to the quality of the available job opportunities outside of teaching. Because college graduates trained in chemistry and physics can earn particularly high salaries in business and industry, those who enter teaching have short first teaching spells and,

Table 6.1 Probability of a return to teaching in North Carolina and Michigan within five years of terminating a first teaching spell, by subject specialty.

Subject-area Specialty	North Carolina	Michigan
Elementary	.29	.31
Secondary	.24	.24
Social studies	.28	.29
Biology	.26	.22
English	.23	.25
Mathematics	.21	.21
Chemistry/physics	.16	.17

Source: Table B.9, Models 6.2 and 6.3, and Table B.10, Models 6.5 and 6.6.

once they quit, they are relatively unlikely to return. Still, the return of one in eight chemistry and physics teachers is not negligible, and appears to reflect the continuing attraction of teaching for some people who could make more money doing something else.

Teachers with Higher Test Scores Are Less Likely to Return

In North Carolina—the state in which we know teachers' scores on the NTE—former teachers who scored high on the NTE were less likely to return than former teachers with lower scores. Of teachers who scored at the 10th percentile on the NTE, for instance, one out of three former teachers reentered teaching within five years of leaving. By contrast, only about one out of every four former teachers with a score at the 90th percentile returned.[15]

This phenomenon is consistent with the findings that high-scoring college graduates are less likely to enter teaching than are lower-scoring graduates, and that high-scoring teachers had shorter first spells than did low-scoring teachers. Together, these patterns demonstrate that our children are increasingly likely to be taught by the academically weakest of the nation's college graduates. In the next chapter we discuss how changes in licensing requirements might alter this trend.

The Reserve Pool in the Future

Will the reserve pool be an important source of teacher supply in the years ahead, as it has been in the past? There will certainly continue to be large numbers of college graduates, mostly women, who have obtained teaching licenses but are not currently teaching. Thus the potential supply will continue to exist. But these graduates will be less likely than their predecessors of twenty years ago to be out of the labor force. Instead, they are likely to be working full time in other sectors of the economy. The education sector will need to compete for their services. Salaries and working conditions will surely influence the number of people working in other sectors of the economy who make the decision to return to teaching. Another factor will be the cost of making such a career switch. In this regard, the increasingly common requirement that teachers earn a master's degree within a short time after beginning to teach may be a significant deterrent to those considering a change in careers.

The lesson here is the importance of evaluating the impact of state and local requirements for becoming a teacher not only on the career choices of college students making occupational choices for the first time, but also on the career choices of graduates working in other sectors of the economy. Given the relatively small number of students who will complete college in the 1990s (the baby bust generation), and the large number of students who completed college in the 1970s and early 1980s (the baby boom generation), providing all children with skilled teachers in the 1990s will require success in attracting a large number of the latter group into teaching.

7

Revising Licensing Requirements

As we have seen, licensing regulations, and prospective teachers' responses to them, directly influence who teaches in the schools. In the 1980s, many states altered licensing requirements. Some added more educational requirements; others instituted tests of applicants' knowledge or skills, or raised the minimum acceptable score on a test already being used. Some states introduced alternative licensing paths, requiring only that applicants pass a test of subject-matter knowledge and participate in an internship program during their first years in the classroom.

Can changes in licensing requirements help schools obtain skilled teachers? If so, what types of licensing requirements would best promote this goal? We begin to answer these questions by examining the economic theory of occupational licensing. This framework reveals the ways in which conventional licensing requirements actually hinder the hiring of skilled teachers. We argue that revised requirements could promote better teaching in our schools, and we describe the new directions requirements should take.

The Economics of Occupational Licensing

State governments license more than eight hundred occupations, including medicine, the law, beekeeping, barbering, and cosmetology.[1] Under most licensing statutes, individuals who do not hold a valid license cannot legally sell their services to consumers. Licensing laws vary among states and among occupations, but they typically create three types of requirements that applicants must meet: completing prescribed training, achieving a score above a prespecified cutoff on a pencil-and-paper test of skills or knowledge, and/or demonstrating competent performance of the work done by practitioners of the occupation.

Occupational licensing protects unwary consumers from incompetent service providers. The importance of this benefit depends on how easily consumers can learn about the quality of the service being sold, and on the damage that could result from unknowingly purchasing a service of lower quality. The benefits of licensing some occupations are small because consumers can collect reasonable information about quality in the absence of regulation, and the cost of making a mistake is modest. Consumers can easily evaluate barbers' work, for example, by observing haircuts given to other customers; and the damage that results from making a mistake is limited to looking unkempt for a few weeks. By contrast, consumers cannot collect reliable information about the quality of heart surgeons' work, and the cost of making a mistake can be loss of life. There is thus considerable value in licensing heart surgeons if the licensing procedures keep incompetent surgeons out of the operating room.

Economists emphasize that the benefits of occupational licensing must be compared with the costs, which are of three major types. First, licensing restricts the supply of service providers, thereby raising the price consumers pay for the service. This occurs because some individuals who could provide the service competently will not bear the costs of the prescribed training program or cannot pass the standardized pencil-and-paper licensing examination. Second, occupational licensing often hinders innovation in training. Regulations that require applicants to complete prescribed programs provide training institutions with captive audiences. This reduces market pressure to improve these programs. Institutions may be reluctant to experiment with radical changes in curriculum for fear that the state may not approve the innovative program, leading to declines in student enrollments when it becomes known that graduates are not being granted licenses.[2] Third, the administrative costs are high, especially if the requirements include a significant amount of evaluation. Consumers ultimately bear a large share of this expense, either through tax payments (if the state bears the administration costs) or through increased service prices (if the state passes on the costs to applicants).

Deciding whether an occupation should be licensed and, if so, what the licensing requirements should be involves a comparison of benefits and costs. For many occupations, licensing laws are unwarranted because the associated costs are high relative to the benefits. When licensure is merited, the challenge is to design requirements that adequately protect consumers at modest cost.

Why Traditional Licensing Requirements for Teachers Are Flawed

Traditionally, a college graduate becomes licensed to teach a particular subject or a particular grade span by completing a state-approved teacher training program offered by a four-year college or university. Programs obtain state approval by demonstrating that they offer, and require students to complete, a series of courses covering material specified by the state. The programs typically include courses on the foundations of education, teaching methods for the particular subject specialty, curriculum development, and child psychology.[3] Thirty-five states also require that applicants score above a prespecified level on one or more multiple-choice tests of particular types of knowledge.[4] Although such conventional licensing requirements undoubtedly prevent some incompetent people from teaching, on balance, they do not promote the goal of staffing all schools with skilled teachers.

Training requirements and the occupational decisions of talented college students

Extensive preservice training requirements deter many talented college students who would like to teach from ever doing so. Some never teach because they attend colleges that do not offer accredited teacher training programs, a lack that prevents students from pursuing a late-developing interest in teaching. Others, who do attend schools with approved programs, never teach because the required preservice courses appear dull and unrelated to the job of teaching and because completing the requirements reduces opportunities to take courses in other fields, including the liberal arts and business. Students may be reluctant to forgo classes that would enhance their competitive position in applying for other jobs if they decide to leave teaching.

Although we will never know exactly how many talented college students decide not to teach because of training requirements, we do know (from Chapter 3) that academically talented college graduates are less likely to teach than are their less talented peers. We also know that private schools (in which graduates can teach without licenses in most states) hire college graduates with higher test scores, on average, than do public schools.[5] As will be discussed later in this chapter, alternative licensing programs in which college graduates without undergraduate teacher training can become teachers also attract graduates with higher test scores, on average, than do traditional training programs. Therefore, even in the absence of clear linkage, we conclude that many talented college students who would like to try teaching *are* deterred by extensive preservice training requirements.

Is this a serious concern? Some observers think not. They argue that the public policy goal is to train teachers who will spend their entire careers in education. From this perspective, it is of little concern that preservice teacher education requirements deter some people from teaching for a number of years before moving on. We disagree. In a society with abundant opportunities for talented college graduates and a tradition of labor market mobility, it will never be possible to persuade two million of them to teach their whole lives. Public rhetoric that implies personal failure when a teacher leaves the classroom after successfully teaching for a number of years may deter many of them from ever setting foot in a classroom.

Many dedicated teachers do spend their entire careers in teaching. Our schools depend on such teachers. But given even the most optimistic projections of teacher salary increases, there will never be enough skilled career teachers to staff the nation's schools. We must find ways to attract more talented college graduates to teaching, to help them learn the skills needed to teach effectively, and to induce them to stay long enough, at least four to five years, to make a significant contribution.

One hypothetical rebuttal to this argument is that only extensive preservice classroom-based teacher education provides prospective teachers with the skills to teach effectively. If so, then even if traditional preservice training does deter some potentially effective college graduates from entering teaching, this cost must be borne in order to provide teachers with needed skills. But there is no evidence that teachers who graduate from accredited training programs are more effective in teaching students than teachers who do not.[6] As we explain in the next section, this does not mean that high-quality preservice training cannot enhance prospective teachers' skills. It means only that mandating training programs with specific content does not contribute to the objective of staffing the schools with skilled teachers.

Test-score requirements and the occupational
decisions of Black college students

The standardized tests most commonly included in teacher licensing requirements are the NTE tests, developed by Educational Testing Service. The NTE tests include a "Core Battery," which includes tests of communication skills, general knowledge, and professional knowledge; forty-nine specialty-area tests, which measure knowledge of specific academic subjects or fields; and the Pre-Professional Skills Tests, which measure basic reading, writing, and mathematics skills.[7] As of 1989, eighteen states used the Core Battery in their teacher licensing requirements. Fifteen states required that applicants for a teaching license in a particular field score above a prespecified cutoff on the relevant NTE specialty-area exam.[8] Twenty-five states required that applicants for admission to undergraduate teacher education programs score above a prespecified cutoff on a standardized test. Seven of these use the Pre-Professional Skills Tests; the other eighteen use other standardized multiple-choice tests, such as the Scholastic Aptitude Test or the California Achievement Test.

These test-score requirements dramatically reduce the number of Black college graduates who obtain teaching licenses, for three related reasons. First, the average scores of Black applicants on these multiple-choice tests are at least one standard deviation below the average scores of White applicants. Second, cutoff scores are set at a level such that the majority of White applicants qualify, and a significant percentage of Black applicants do not.[9] Third, aware of these patterns, many Black college students decide not to prepare to teach.

The use of standardized multiple-choice tests in teacher licensing programs is extremely controversial. Part of the controversy stems from the very low correlation between scores on these tests and measures of teaching effectiveness. In 1987 a comprehensive review concluded: "The available evidence is none too good, but it indicates that teacher tests have little, if any, power to predict how well people perform as teachers, whether that performance is judged by ratings of college supervisory personnel, ratings by teachers, student ratings, or achievement gains made by students."[10]

Defenders of the use of these tests argue that the lack of correlation between test scores and measures of teaching effectiveness is not the issue. They argue that the tests screen out applicants who lack the basic literacy, numeracy, and writing skills to serve as successful role models to students and to write grammatically correct, coherent letters to parents. This argument has some merit. All teachers should write and speak coherent English. And taxpayers must know that there are "standards" for becoming a teacher if they are to support the salary increases needed to attract and retain effective teachers.

But the core issue is whether the use of multiple-choice tests in state licensing procedures increases the likelihood that our nation's children will be taught by effective teachers of varying backgrounds. There are several reasons to question whether multiple-choice tests help achieve this goal. First, items assessing "general knowledge" inevitably reflect to some extent the majority White culture, and this is one reason Black applicants tend to score lower than White applicants on such tests. Second, multiple-choice tests of "professional knowledge," which are part of the licensing requirements in twenty-four states,[11] do not measure reliably whether applicants possess the knowledge needed to teach effectively, because the test items rarely provide the rich contextual information needed to respond thoughtfully to a problem situation. Nor do multiple-choice questions allow applicants to offer creative responses. Such limitations are critical. Recent research has shown that the correct answer to almost all questions about how a teacher should respond in a particular classroom situation is: "It depends."[12] The National Commission on Testing and Public Policy commented in its 1990 report: "questions on teacher certification tests that survived . . . scrutiny over the years have been roundly criticized by subsequent test reviewers as simplistic, containing professional shibboleths, having a shaky research base, or measuring trivial content."[13] Third, use of the professional knowledge test provides the wrong set of incentives to applicants. Instead of learning to teach effectively, applicants with low scores devote attention to learning the "correct" answers.[14] We doubt that hours spent in learning to pass multiple-choice tests of professional knowledge improve the quality of teaching.

Given the lack of evidence relating scores on multiple-choice tests of knowledge to measures of teaching effectiveness, how has the use of these tests survived legal challenge? The courts have ruled that use of the NTE tests in licensing is justified because they measure "the content of the academic preparation of prospective teachers."[15] In other words, the defense is that the tests measure particular types of knowledge and are not intended to measure teaching effectiveness. This is a weak defense, indeed, given the questionable validity of multiple-choice questions about professional knowledge and given the demonstrably negative impact that the test-score requirements have on the racial composition of the teaching force.

A challenge in revising licensing requirements is to find a way to ensure that potential teachers do possess the skills to communicate effectively with students and their parents, and to do so in a manner that is sensitive to cultural diversity and that provides incentives and opportunities for candidates deficient in basic skills.

Why Licensing of Teachers Is Necessary

Conventional licensing requirements are flawed because their benefits are extremely modest relative to their costs. What changes in licensing requirements would improve the balance between benefits and costs? One option is to reduce licensing requirements dramatically, requiring only that potential licensees graduate from a four-year college or university. We do not recommend this change, for several reasons. First, the quality of instruction and the graduation standards of the nation's 2,100 four-year colleges and universities vary widely. Possession of a bachelor's degree does not guarantee that a graduate has attained a solid understanding of a discipline or even that the graduate has solid literacy and numeracy skills.

Weaknesses in the skills of many college graduates would not justify restrictive licensure requirements if every school district sought teachers who were capable of helping children to learn, had the resources and skills to recruit a strong applicant pool, and had the skills to screen applicants thoroughly. If every district were as capable as the Grandview district described in Chapter 4, state licensing of applicants for teaching positions would be unnecessary. But we know that many districts' screening procedures do not reliably identify which candidates have literacy skills, subject-matter competence, and teaching skills. We doubt that the centralized screening procedures used in the Harteville district described in Chapter 4, for example, can reliably distinguish strong applicants from weaker ones.

Part of this problem stems from inadequate school financing. Effective personnel procedures require significant resources. Even more important, good procedures will yield an effective teaching force only if the applicant pool contains skilled teachers. Low salary schedules and poor working conditions do not attract competent teachers. In some districts, salaries and working conditions are uncompetitive because the tax base is so small that even relatively high property tax rates cannot raise enough revenue to support competitive salaries; in other districts, residents are unwilling to pay the taxes necessary for a strong school program.

The aging of the population, which reduces the percentage of voters with children of school age, exacerbates these problems. Older citizens, many of whom live on fixed incomes, are less likely to vote for local tax increases than are voters with children who have not completed school.[16]

Licensing requirements that prevent local districts from hiring unskilled teachers will not, by themselves, improve the teaching force. Salaries and working conditions that good teachers find attractive are necessary conditions for recruiting skilled teachers. But to the extent that licensing requirements result in unfilled vacancies in districts unable to hire qualified teachers, they highlight the inadequacies of public education in these school districts and underscore the need for significant change.

A final problem with eliminating licensing requirements entirely is that some school districts treat teaching positions as jobs to be doled out to supporters of the local government. A series of articles in the *New York Times* in 1989 documented such abuses in several of New York's decentralized community school districts.[17] Opposing patronage is rarely cited as a reason for state licensing requirements for teachers. Concerns about local government personnel practices, nevertheless, continue to be a motivation for such requirements.

An unconventional case for licensing

Conventional economic theory assumes that the consumer is competent and has the right priorities, but simply lacks information. Licensing, if merited, is a response to this information gap. We offer a different argument for state licensing of public school teachers, one that rests on the notion that some local school districts (the purchasers of teachers' services) are underfunded, incompetent, or have priorities that the state finds unacceptable. Debates about licensing requirements for teachers typically ignore such an argument, because legislators fear political disadvantage in admitting that local officials are incompetent or corrupt or that voters' priorities are suspect. Yet these issues must be raised. If poor information were the only problem, policy could focus on improving information about candidates' strengths and weaknesses. States could require that prospective teachers be tested on their knowledge of the appropriate subject matter and that the scores be part of applicants' resumes. Local districts could then decide how to use this information in making hiring decisions. In other words, the state's role would be to improve the information about job candidates available to local districts, not to restrict the hiring decisions of local districts.

Limiting the choices of local districts is justified only by recognizing that, even with improved information, some districts will hire teachers whom the state finds unacceptable. States are concerned because equal opportunity is threatened when incompetent teachers are hired, and the costs of inadequate education are borne not only by the children themselves and local residents but also by the larger society. Dimensions of these costs include a lower rate of economic growth,[18] higher incidence of welfare, greater crime rates, and higher unemployment rates.[19]

If licensing can reduce the number of children taught by ineffective teachers, this is an important social benefit. The challenge is to design new licensing requirements that are more effective in upholding minimum standards, and that impose fewer costs.

Evidence Informing the Redesign of Licensing Requirements

Two types of evidence are particularly useful in planning the redesign of licensing requirements. The first concerns New Jersey's experiences with an alternative path to teaching. The second concerns recent research on the knowledge base underlying effective teaching.

New Jersey's Provisional Teacher Program

In 1984 New Jersey initiated the Provisional Teacher Program, which provides an alternative to the conventional path for becoming a public school teacher in the state. The requirements to enter this program are a bachelor's degree, a thirty-credit major in the field in which the person would teach (prospective elementary school teachers may major in any field), and a passing score on the appropriate NTE specialty-area test. No preservice training is necessary.[20]

Entering Provisional Teachers must complete a three-part, one-year program to qualify for a permanent teaching license. During this internship year, participants serve as regular classroom teachers. Before assuming charge of a classroom, Provisional Teachers spend twenty days in an "initial teaching experience" under the supervision of an experienced teacher. During the school year, they complete a training program that includes two hundred hours of formal instruction in the knowledge and skills needed to teach effectively. Experienced teachers supervise and support the Provisional Teachers. Only districts that demonstrate the capacity to administer this year-long training and supervision program may hire Provisional Teachers.

Three times during the school year, local district officials evaluate the performance of each Provisional Teacher. The first two evaluations provide advice. The third evaluation determines whether the Provisional Teacher receives a permanent teaching license, valid in any New Jersey school district.[21]

Participants in the Provisional Teacher Program pay fees totaling $1,400 (as of 1989) for the in-service training they receive. They also receive a salary during their initial year of teaching that is at least as high as the state's minimum teacher salary of $18,500.[22]

Data are now available that describe the teachers who completed the New Jersey Provisional Teacher Program during its first five years of operation. The program has become an increasingly important source of teacher supply in the state. In 1985, 114 Provisional Teachers began work in New Jersey public schools. In 1989, 276 Provisional Teachers did so—a number that represents 24 percent of all beginning teachers hired by the state's public schools during that school year.[23]

The growing number of college graduates entering public school teaching through the Provisional Teacher Program supports our argument that there are many college graduates who would like to teach, but are deterred by traditional preservice training requirements. The Provisional Teacher Program has become a significant supply source for teachers of physical sciences, areas of teacher shortage in many states. In 1989, the Provisional Teacher Program produced forty-two qualified applicants in chemistry or physics, compared with only four who graduated from traditional undergraduate teacher preparation programs.[24] The Provisional Teacher Program applicants, moreover, had especially strong academic skills, achieving an average score of 633 on the NTE physical sciences examination, compared with an average score of 562 for the graduates of the traditional training programs.[25]

The Provisional Teacher Program has also attracted many minority teachers. Twenty-one percent of the 1,506 teachers who entered New Jersey public and private schools through this program between 1985 and 1989 were minority group members, a percentage more than twice as high as the percentage of minority group members among graduates of traditional undergraduate teacher training programs in the state.[26] This pattern is particularly striking because the Provisional Teacher Program requires that applicants achieve quite high scores on the NTE. This suggests that many minority group members are deterred from becoming teachers, not by test-score requirements, but by undergraduate training requirements. Creating alternative paths into teaching may help attract more talented minority group members to the profession.[27]

A final piece of encouraging news from the New Jersey Provisional Teacher Program is that the first-year attrition rate of Provisional Teachers is lower than the first-year attrition rate of teachers trained in traditional undergraduate programs, and lower than the first-year attrition rates we found in Michigan and North Carolina. Only 5 percent of the Provisional Teachers who began teaching in New Jersey schools during the first four years of the program left either during or after their first year of teaching. The comparable figure for beginning teachers trained in traditional undergraduate programs is 18 percent.[28] This finding alleviates the fear that college graduates who enter teaching without undergraduate teacher education will be so overwhelmed by problems that they will quickly resign.

The key lesson we take from the New Jersey experience is that there are a substantial number of academically talented college graduates who would like to teach, but are deterred from doing so by conventional undergraduate training requirements. Evidence on "alternative route" teacher licensing programs in other states supports this conclusion.[29]

No single program, however, will solve the problem of staffing the schools. Many routes into teaching are needed. In addition, many questions about the New Jersey program remain. Critics argue that the quality of the in-service training and supervision received by program participants is often low, and that novice teachers are ill equipped to grapple with the demands of students.[30] Although we know of no systematic data evaluating this claim, we have little doubt that the quality of support varies. Developing and sustaining effective mentorship programs for novice teachers is a problem in all settings. Alternative route programs may be particularly vulnerable to this problem because participants have little or no practice teaching experience. This limitation must be balanced, however, against the success many alternative route programs have in attracting academically talented college graduates to teaching.

The implications of new research on teacher education

Recent research on teaching has progressed beyond the traditional search for generic teacher behaviors that enhance student learning to a systematic search for the types of knowledge teachers need to have and be able to use to teach effectively. Lee Shulman, one of the central figures in the search for a richer knowledge base for teaching, argues compellingly that pedagogical knowledge does not consist of a set of skills apart from subject matter knowledge. In his words, "the key to distinguishing the knowledge base of teaching lies at the intersection of content and pedagogy, in the capacity of a teacher to transform the content knowledge he or she possesses into forms that are pedagogically powerful and yet adaptive to the variations in ability and background presented by the students."[31]

Shulman also argues that, although much of the knowledge base for effective teaching is still to be discovered, enough is known to demonstrate convincingly that knowledge of the subject matter is not enough to teach effectively. In his words, "our question should not be, Is there really much one needs to know in order to teach? Rather, it should express our wonder at how the extensive knowledge of teaching can be learned at all during the brief period allotted to teacher preparation."[32]

Shulman is no apologist for traditional teacher education programs. He argues that the emerging conception of a knowledge base requires dramatic revision of both the organization and the content of teacher education programs. Instruction in pedagogy and supervision cannot be separated from the study of subject matter, as has traditionally been the case in preservice teacher education programs.[33] What form should these revisions take? The evidence bearing on this question is extremely thin. The work of one of Shulman's colleagues, Pamela Grossman, indicates that high-quality university-based preservice teacher education that focuses on how to teach particular subjects can influence how novice teachers teach.[34] In other words, preservice training can make a difference. But Grossman studied novice teachers who attended a small program housed in a major research university and who undoubtedly had very different preservice training than most aspiring teachers experience.

The state can mandate that teachers graduate from preservice training programs and can specify the material that must be covered in these programs. But no set of requirements can guarantee that the material will be taught well enough to benefit program participants or to attract more academically able students than most preservice training programs have in recent years. This reality underlies some of our suggestions for changes in teacher licensing requirements.

Directions for New Licensing Requirements

We draw two conclusions from the New Jersey Provisional Teacher Program and the recent research on the knowledge base underlying effective teaching. First, relaxing traditional preservice training requirements will attract more talented college graduates to teaching. Second, high-calibre teacher training can help prospective teachers teach more effectively. The challenge, then, is to design licensing requirements that draw talented college graduates to teaching and create incentives for these graduates to search out and complete training programs that provide them with the skills they need to teach effectively.

In our view, an effective strategy for achieving these objectives has three parts. The first is a test of literacy and writing skills that all applicants for teacher training programs must pass. The second is the creation of many alternative training programs. The third is a system of high-quality assessments of teaching performance that novice teachers must pass in order to obtain a long-term teaching license.

*A test of literacy and writing skills (and a caution
about subject-matter knowledge tests)*

The need for a test of literacy and writing skills stems from the enormous variation in the graduation standards of the nation's high schools and colleges. Degrees do not guarantee competence, and there can be no doubt all of the nation's children should be taught by teachers who can communicate effectively with children and their parents.

The design and administration of this test should adhere to four principles. First, the test should involve "constructed responses," in which applicants carry out tasks similar to those that teachers do as part of their jobs. For example, prospective candidates might be asked to write a letter to parents explaining plans for a field trip. Second, the content of the test should be made public after each administration. This provides applicants with information needed to prepare efficiently for the test, and it facilitates public debate on whether the test assesses skills all teachers should have. Third, the responses should be graded by committees with adequate representation of minority group members who can detect differences in language usage stemming from cultural differences. Fourth, applicants should be able to take the test early in their own academic careers, as early as high school, when remediation is easiest. Adherence to these principles should ensure that newly licensed teachers do possess basic literacy and writing skills, while providing opportunities for aspiring teachers from all backgrounds to acquire the skills needed to pass the test.

We find compelling the arguments of Shulman and his colleagues that knowledge of the subject matter is necessary to teach well. In principle, assessing the subject-matter knowledge of candidates for teaching licenses makes sense. We have doubts, however, about whether the multiple-choice tests currently used in twenty-three states validly assess subject-matter knowledge.[35] Consider the criticisms many scientists and science educators raise about the use of multiple-choice tests to measure student knowledge of science. (To our knowledge, no similar analyses of the NTE specialty-area tests have been conducted.) These critics point out that multiple-choice items may fail to test science knowledge in several ways: they may measure general knowledge and consequently be more indicative of IQ than of science knowledge; they may measure skill in ruling out multiple-choice options; they may reflect a simplistic view of science. As part of a National Research Council evaluation of educational indicators, one committee member conducted a review of the released test questions from the National Assessment of Educational Progress's science tests for 9-year-olds and 13-year-olds: one third of the questions were seriously deficient.[36]

Given the problems in designing valid multiple-choice tests of science knowledge, we recommend extreme caution in assessing the subject-matter knowledge of candidates for teaching licenses. In our view, the long-term solution is to design constructed response tests that provide more valid measures of subject-matter knowledge than multiple-choice tests do. The administration and grading costs may be higher, but these costs seem modest relative to the high costs of either licensing teachers without critically needed knowledge or failing to license teachers who possess the subject knowledge needed to teach well, but do not perform well on multiple-choice tests.

In the interim, states should release large random samples of items used on multiple-choice tests of subject-matter knowledge. The ensuing public scrutiny would improve the quality of the debate about teacher licensing requirements. Any test that cannot withstand this debate should be eliminated from the process of determining who can teach in the nation's schools.

A variety of training programs

If university-based preservice training of high quality can improve teaching performance, why do we recommend the creation of alternatives to this traditional path into teaching? First, requiring that all candidates complete particular courses creates a captive audience for the institutions and faculty providing these courses. This significantly reduces incentives to improve instruction. Required courses are often dull and of little value. Second, state requirements that mandated courses cover particular topics can hamper innovation in the design of teacher education. Third, no single training strategy is best for all potential teachers. This is particularly true as the average age of new entrants increases, a pattern documented in Chapters 2 and 3. An increasing proportion of potential teachers have done work after college in which they have learned some of the skills needed for effective teaching. The mother who has raised several children and run a variety of volunteer programs for children probably has acquired significant classroom management skills. The army sergeant who has spent several years as an instructor in an electronics school may have learned many of the skills involved in helping students learn mathematics. It is undoubtedly true that both of these potential teachers have a great deal to learn before they can teach effectively. But what they need to learn may differ, and the type of program that will be most effective in providing them with the needed skills may differ as well.

A goal of public policy should be to encourage the development of creative, high-quality strategies for teacher training and to provide incentives for talented college students to learn the skills needed to teach competently. A system of performance assessments that aspiring teachers must pass in order to obtain a long-term teaching license is the key to achieving this goal.

A system of licensing assessments coupled with the development of a variety of alternative training options creates two sets of desirable incentives. Gone are the captive audiences and the constraints on the design of teacher training programs. Individuals and organizations with good ideas about how to train teachers could develop programs and try to attract students. Groups interested in designing training programs might include not only education faculty at colleges and universities but also teachers in public schools, private schools, and even private organizations. School districts could offer internships in which candidates would work with experienced teachers to learn critical skills. Other groups could schedule training programs in the evening to appeal to the large group of baby boomers between the ages of 30 and 45 who might like to enter teaching if they could prepare for the assessment while continuing to hold their current positions. Still other providers might offer intensive courses for academically talented college graduates who can learn rapidly. The presence of a demanding performance assessment and the absence of mandated training requirements should foster innovative training strategies.

The availability of multiple paths creates a second set of desirable incentives in that individuals interested in public school teaching would search for ways to acquire the skills needed to pass the licensing assessment. This search would lead them to ask about program costs and about the percentage of the graduates of particular training programs who obtain licenses. High-quality performance assessments would reveal whether the brief summer training and the mentor-led in-service training provided to participants in "alternate route" programs such as New Jersey's Provisional Teacher Program effectively provide aspiring teachers with critical skills. Performance-based licensing would serve as a check on the quality of the in-service training provided by individual school districts. Districts in which a significant proportion of the Provisional Teachers failed the assessment could be prohibited from employing Provisional Teachers.

Trade-offs in the Design of Performance Assessments

We are convinced that using performance assessments to license teachers will improve the quality of teachers in the nation's schools. But it is far from easy to develop high-quality performance assessments and to implement systems of licensure based on them. Meeting these challenges will require large investments, a sustained research effort, and considerable experimentation.

How should performance be assessed?

Educational researchers have proposed a variety of strategies for assessing the skills of novice teachers. Some involve evaluation by trained observers of the candidates at work with students. Others involve evaluating candidates' written responses to simulated problems. Each strategy has strengths and limitations. The attraction of evaluating teachers as they work with students is clear; after all, this is the task of teaching. But a candidate's success in working with students depends heavily on factors beyond her control, such as the composition of the student body and the availability of materials, supplies, and support at the school site. Two equally capable novice teachers might appear to differ markedly in effectiveness as a result of nothing more than differences in work contexts.

Pencil-and-paper assessments have different strengths and limitations. On the positive side, they dramatically reduce differences in context. Every candidate for licensure in a particular teaching area is assessed by the same standard. Such evaluations are also considerably less expensive to administer than classroom-based assessments. But standardized assessments will never capture variations in critical dimensions of teaching skill, such as teachers' responses to unpredicted student questions and demands.

There is no single right answer to the question of how best to assess candidates' teaching skills. Nor is it clear how much training of evaluators and/or use of technologies such as videotaping can reduce the trade-off between realism and consistency. A number of research teams are working on these and related questions, as we shall describe later in this chapter.

How high should the minimum performance level be set?

Setting a high performance standard for licensure has the potential benefit of eliciting support for relatively high teacher salaries—a necessary condition for attracting large numbers of talented college graduates to teaching. State officials can defend salary increases by arguing that the high standards ensure that only highly skilled teachers are granted licenses. If maintained, high standards can also ensure that school districts dominated by patronage do not hire candidates who have better political connections than teaching skills.

A high standard also creates difficulties. If too few candidates earn licensure, political support for these standards will decline. If a high standard leads to teacher shortages, there will be strong pressures for exceptions—that is, permission for local districts to hire unlicensed teachers "on an emergency basis." As exceptions cumulate, they eliminate the value of performance-based licensing.

Much remains to be learned about the consequences of setting different levels of performance standards. Experience will help states evaluate, for example, how high salaries must be to provide an adequate supply of candidates capable of satisfying a stringent performance standard, and which parts of performance assessments prove most problematic for novice teachers.

When should the performance of candidates for licensure be assessed?

Most analysts agree that teachers really begin to learn to teach only when they encounter students in regular classroom situations, and that even high-quality preservice training cannot substitute for learning on the job. This suggests that performance should be assessed only after novice teachers have had time to learn to teach, perhaps after a period of at least one year if not two. Some aspiring teachers, however, never acquire the skills to teach effectively, and it is important to remove these individuals from classrooms as soon as possible. The longer incompetent teachers remain in the classroom, the greater the cost to students.

As with the other difficult issues in designing assessments, much remains to be learned. Little is known, for example, about the extent to which the damage to children from delayed assessments of incompetent novice teachers can be mitigated by careful supervision by mentors, or the extent to which preservice tests of basic skills and subject knowledge screen out potentially ineffective teachers. Only as evidence collects from state experiences with performance-based assessments will the consequences of alternative strategies become more clear.

The National Board for Professional Teaching Standards

In 1986, the Carnegie Task Force on Teaching as a Profession called for the establishment of a National Board for Professional Teaching Standards (NBPTS). The new organization, which began work in 1987, has the mandate to create a corps of experienced "Board Certified teachers" who have demonstrated superior competence by passing a rigorous performance assessment.[37]

There are many questions about the consequences of the NBPTS's activities. Will Board Certified teachers be in high demand? How much additional income will they command? Will the assessments reflect the special difficulties of teaching in urban schools, and will skilled minority group teachers working in these schools apply for Board Certification? Answers to these questions will not be known for years to come.

Although application for Board Certification is voluntary and is not designed to replace state licensing of teachers, the work of the NBPTS may dramatically affect the development of state performance-based licensing systems. The NBPTS is sponsoring a great deal of research on alternative assessment approaches.[38] This will increase the knowledge base on which states can draw in designing assessment strategies. If Board Certified teachers are highly sought as exemplary practitioners, parents may argue that all of their children's teachers should meet these same standards. This would strengthen the constituency for performance-based licensing and build support for the taxes needed to establish and maintain a teaching force of high quality.

Alternative Assessment Approaches

In recent years a number of research groups have proposed alternative strategies for assessing teachers' skills. Some of these groups are working under contract to the NBPTS; others are working in conjunction with state Departments of Education that seek performance-based licensing. To illustrate the range of possibilities and the difficult trade-offs in design, we describe three strategies and compare their strengths and limitations.[39]

The RAND strategy: Task simulations

Researchers at the RAND Corporation are developing pencil-and-paper assessments of teaching skills for the state of California. The RAND group is designing simulation problems that can be used to assess candidates' skills in four areas: instruction, planning, evaluation and assessment, and classroom management. Each candidate may be asked to construct responses to several structured simulation problems in a four- to six-hour period. (Note that these tasks are very different from completing multiple-choice tests.) Each description includes a rich set of information about the teaching context in which the task is set. Candidates for licensure in English, for example, may be asked to take a set of resource materials and plan a sequence of lessons that meets particular curricular goals, for a class of students with particular backgrounds and skills. They may then be asked to evaluate a set of essays written by students in another class. Background materials again include information about the students and the purposes of the assignment. Candidates may be asked to "(1) make constructive comments on each paper to assist the students in revising their papers, (2) indicate the common problem(s) exhibited by the set of papers as a group, and (3) describe briefly what should be done to correct the common problem(s) in forthcoming lessons and/or homework assignments."[40]

The ETS strategy: Classroom observation

The Educational Testing Service is redesigning the NTE tests. The new generation of assessments will have three parts: tests of basic reading, mathematics, and writing skills (the first two of which will involve short answers typed into computers), tests of subject-matter knowledge (which will include questions requiring open-ended responses as well as multiple-choice questions), and methods for measuring the classroom performance of beginning teachers.[41] We focus on the last of these three parts.

The ETS plan is to rely primarily on classroom observations for measuring a teacher's performance. Trained observers will focus their evaluations on four content areas: planning for instruction, implementation of instruction, classroom management, and evaluating students' progress. Of particular concern will be the extent to which teachers adapt their behaviors to fit the particular classroom situation, as defined by four context variables: students' individual differences, cultural backgrounds, and developmental levels, and the subject matter being taught.[42] ETS recommends that each candidate be observed several times. ETS will not administer these performance assessments; it will provide technical assistance to states in training observers, developing scoring strategies, and setting minimum performance standards. Postobservation interviews and written responses to predesignated questions may supplement the observations. The central assumption underlying the ETS strategy is that trained evaluators' observations of a teacher working with students provide the most valid and reliable means of assessing his or her teaching skills.

Collins and Frederiksen: A focus on teacher-student interactions

The cognitive scientists Allan Collins and John Frederiksen propose a strategy for assessing teaching skills that is similar to the ETS approach in that it focuses on observing teachers at work with students. What is particularly interesting in Collins and Frederiksen's assessment strategy is that it focuses on both the teacher and the students, and on their interactions. Collins and Frederiksen argue that in a classroom where effective teaching is taking place, students talk about what they do, reflect, and articulate theories and frame questions. Students help each other and engage in collaborative problem solving. Everyone is involved, weaker students as well as stronger students, girls as well as boys.[43] Important aspects of effective teaching, as these researchers envision it, are to listen carefully and to set up activities through which students learn from each other. This approach is sometimes characterized as "teacher as coach." Collins and Frederiksen believe that trained assessors can judge teaching competency reliably by watching a teacher at work with students or, even better, by watching a videotape of a teacher and students at work.

A comparison of alternative assessment strategies

A major strength of Collins and Frederiksen's approach and the ETS approach is that they involve observation of teachers working with students—the fundamental mission teachers carry out every day. Basing licensing decisions on an assessment of the extent to which applicants can do the work they are hired to do has great appeal.

A tension that Collins and Frederiksen and the ETS research group face concerns the model of effective teaching that underlies the design of their assessments. Both groups want their assessments to drive practice in desirable directions, and they recognize that this can happen only if the assessments are based on an explicit model of effective teaching. At the same time, both groups recognize that effective teachers adapt their behaviors to the classroom situations. Thus, they must design assessment instruments that rest on explicit models of effective teaching, and that are sufficiently flexible to recognize that competent teaching can assume quite different forms in different classroom situations. It is too early to judge whether assessment procedures can be devised that keep this tension manageable.

A related problem with assessment approaches focusing on observing teachers at work is that teachers' evaluations may depend critically on the personalities and backgrounds of their students. These will vary among classrooms and schools, and consequently the "difficulty" of the examination will vary among candidates for licensure. Such variation in difficulty may be inappropriate in a crucial licensing examination.[44]

The dependence of the "difficulty" of the teaching examination on a teacher's students is particularly troublesome in light of the evidence we present in Chapter 5 that Black teachers are much more likely to work in urban districts serving high percentages of children from poor families than are White teachers. Since these children are more likely to come to school hungry and with significant skill deficits than are middle-class suburban children, teachers working with these children face a particularly difficult challenge. Basing licensure on the extent to which teachers can motivate their students to engage in the actions that facilitate learning may result in licences being denied to Black candidates at a higher rate than to White candidates. Since Black teachers are more likely to work with students from low-income families than White teachers are, it may be extremely difficult to assess whether a higher failure rate stems from differences in the students and other aspects of the teaching context or from differences in the applicants' teaching skills.

A strength of the constructed response assessments proposed by the RAND Corporation is that every applicant for a teaching license in a particular field will complete the same simulated tasks. This may make it easier for the state to argue that a RAND-style licensing examination treats all applicants fairly than is the case with the ETS and Collins-Frederiksen approaches.[45] But some analysts argue that the RAND approach puts heavy emphasis on analytic skills that are only indirectly related to teaching practice and that are much more characteristic of upper middle-class White culture than of Black culture. If so, the RAND approach may discriminate against Black teachers more than a classroom-based assessment approach.[46] A related question is whether applicants could master the skills needed to do well on the pencil-and-paper assessments, yet still fail as teachers because of an inability to work with students. Finally, any licensing examination based on applicants' constructed responses to simulated problems creates incentives for training institutions to teach only the skills needed to do well on the simulated problems and to neglect other skills that may affect teaching competence, but that cannot be measured reliably on constructed response tests.

At this stage there is not enough evidence to evaluate the relative strengths and limitations of the alternative approaches recommended by Collins and Frederiksen, ETS, and Rand. But these three approaches have common elements that should be part of all licensing examinations. First, applicants should be provided with detailed information on the nature of the assessment and on what constitutes high-quality performance. The RAND group proposes that the tasks used in previous administrations of the licensing examination be made available to applicants along with copies of applicants' responses that were judged to be of high quality. Collins and Frederiksen propose that videotapes of teaching performances in each subject field that are judged to be exemplary be made available to applicants. ETS proposes to provide training materials that will guide beginning teachers' efforts to prepare for the performance assessment.

Second, any assessment must have "systemic validity": the skills measured on the assessments must appear to contribute to effective teaching. A consequence of the evident tie to teaching is that preparing for this part of the licensing examination will help the candidate to be a better teacher.[47] This is a critical property for any test or assessment used in licensing procedures, because applicants will devote valuable time to preparing for it.

A third common element is that all of the research groups involve many classroom teachers in the design and/or review of the assessment strategies. Not only does this contribute to the quality of the assessments—because teachers can judge whether the assessment criteria are consonant with their experiences of what works with students—it also helps in building a constituency for performance-based licensing.

Using Performance Assessments in Teacher Licensing: Evidence from Connecticut

Connecticut has been in the forefront of efforts to introduce performance assessments into teacher licensing procedures. The Connecticut experience teaches us many lessons that may be useful for other states.

The economic and demographic situation

Connecticut is one of the wealthiest states in the nation, with a 1988 per capita income of $23,059, compared with a national average of $16,489.[48] The economic strength of the state throughout the 1980s facilitated the introduction of performance-based licensing procedures because this prosperity provided support for teacher salary increases. In 1988, when the average starting salary in the nation was $19,600, every district in Connecticut had a minimum starting salary of $20,000 or more.[49] By 1990, approximately half of Connecticut districts had starting salaries above $25,000.[50]

These dramatic increases in teacher salaries are relevant to the successful implementation of performance-based licensing in two ways. First, the higher salaries enlarged the pool of candidates for licensure, and increased the likelihood that local districts could attract an adequate supply of candidates who could pass the performance-based licensing examinations. Second, the demanding licensing standards were critical in developing voter support for the salary increases.

Another characteristic of the Connecticut environment favorable to the introduction of performance-based licensing is the relatively low level of demand for new classroom teachers. The stability of student enrollments contributes to the low demand. Connecticut public school enrollment bottomed out in 1988 after seventeen years of decline, and is expected to rise only slowly over the next few years.[51] In addition, school districts tend to fill vacancies by offering positions to members of the reserve pool, mostly former teachers who already hold teaching licenses, rather than to beginning teachers. Fewer than half of the newly hired teachers in 1989 were beginning teachers.

A consequence of the salary increases and the relatively low level of demand for new teachers is that the state Department of Education is not under great pressure to grant exemptions from performance-based licensure to local school districts unable to attract qualified teachers. A large number of exemptions would vitiate the impact of the licensing procedures on the composition of the teaching force.

The assessment components

To teach in a Connecticut public school, candidates for a teaching license must satisfy two "gateway" requirements. The first is an essential skills requirement, which candidates may pass by achieving scores above specified cutoffs on the reading, writing, and mathematics components of the Connecticut Competency Examination for Prospective Teachers (CONNCEPT), or by submitting either a combined score of 1000 or more on the verbal and mathematics subtests of the Scholastic Aptitude Test or a combined score of 24 or more on the American College Testing Program.[52] College students must pass the CONNCEPT before gaining admission to teacher education programs at Connecticut colleges and universities. The second "gateway" requirement is demonstration of subject knowledge. Candidates for licenses in a particular teaching field demonstrate knowledge of the appropriate subject matter by achieving a score above a specified level on the appropriate NTE specialty-area test.[53] The cutscores vary across specialty areas, but tend to be slightly above the average cutscores used by other states and considerably below the cutscores used in licensing teachers in California.[54]

Connecticut made a formal policy decision in 1985 to evaluate professional knowledge only by using performance assessment approaches. Beginning in the 1989–90 school year, every beginning teacher in Connecticut public schools participates in the Beginning Educator Support and Training Program (BEST), which is the third component of Connecticut's licensing requirements. This program provides each novice teacher with a mentor and is designed to help the beginning teacher acquire the skills needed to teach effectively.

During the first teaching year, every novice teacher must undergo classroom-based assessments of teaching skills. Trained assessors observe the teacher at work. There is no presumption that there is one best way to teach. A candidate demonstrates teaching skill by achieving satisfactory scores on evaluations of ten specific teaching competencies, which make up the Connecticut Competency Instrument (CCI). This instrument has been developed by the state Department of Education in collaboration with a large number of Connecticut teachers and other educators.[55] The evaluations (six, in all) of each novice teacher's performance in the classroom are undertaken by state-selected exemplary classroom teachers, administrators, and other educators who have undergone at least fifty hours of training in the CCI criteria and who have been certified as proficient in the conduct of such performance judgments.[56] An assessor does not rate candidates employed by the assessor's home district.

A final planned component of the Connecticut teacher performance assessment is a semistructured interview, to be administered in assessment centers. Novice teachers will be asked questions that probe skill areas, especially their knowledge of how to teach particular subjects. For instance, a novice secondary school mathematics teacher might be shown "samples of student work containing errors in the solution of linear equations. The teacher would be asked to review the student's work and identify the errors the student made and to offer suggestions about why it might have occurred. The teacher might also be asked how the error might be remediated and what might be done to help the student avoid making the error in the future."[57]

Evidence and lessons

Connecticut's experience with performance-based assessments suggests several lessons for other states. The first is that a performance-based licensing system can be implemented if economic and demographic conditions are favorable and if significant resources are devoted to developing the assessment instruments, training the assessors, and administering the system. This evidence is important. Given the history of difficulties in implementing educational reforms in the United States in the past,[58] it has not been obvious that a state government could develop and administer a performance-based licensing system under even the best of circumstances. At the same time, the Connecticut experience suggests that the introduction of performance-based licensing requires a long-term effort and a major financial investment. It is not a quick fix for inadequate quality.

A second lesson concerns the link between teacher training and performance assessments. Most novice teachers who applied for teaching licenses in Connecticut during the 1989–90 school year completed undergraduate teacher training programs, but a small number participated in the Alternate Route Program. College graduates interested in teaching who lack teacher training, but who have a subject matter major and pass the CONNCEPT and the NTE specialty-area test, may apply for admission. Participants engage in eight weeks of intensive training the summer before they take a position as a classroom teacher under the supervision of a mentor teacher. Novice teachers in the Alternate Route Program participate in a district-planned program of supervision, work with a mentor teacher for two years, and undergo the performance-based licensing assessment throughout the two-year period.[59]

Of the relatively small group of beginning teachers who participated in the Alternate Route Program, 75 percent passed all ten dimensions of the Connecticut Competency Instrument. This compares quite favorably with the 88 percent passing rate for teachers who graduated from undergraduate teacher training programs.[60] Connecticut officials emphasize that these results should not be interpreted to mean that no training is needed to pass the teaching competencies assessment. The Alternate Route candidates were very carefully selected for the program, participated in an intensive summer training program, and were given considerable in-service training from their mentors and supervisors during the two-year induction period. But this evidence does support a central argument of this chapter—that undergraduate teacher training is only one of several ways to learn critical teaching skills. Although undergraduate training should remain an option, it should not be the only alternative.

A third lesson concerns the effects of the "gateway" examinations. One effect of such tests is to eliminate from the pool of potential licensees candidates with weak academic skills. In the case of the essential skills requirement, this is done before a candidate even begins teacher training. By strengthening the pool of candidates who subsequently undergo the performance assessments, Connecticut maintains a relatively high passing rate with moderately demanding standards.

A second effect involves minority teachers. Making the achievement of relatively high scores on standardized tests of essential skills (CONNCEPT) a requirement for entry to undergraduate teacher training programs keeps low the number of minority group members who become teachers. In 1988, 5 percent of the students in Connecticut colleges and universities were Black.[61] Yet only 3 percent of the college students who took the CONNCEPT were Black.[62] The passing rates on the CONNCEPT indicate that this test deters many Black students. From 1985 to 1989, only 38 percent of the approximately three hundred Black candidates who took the CONNCEPT passed on the first try, compared with 64 percent of White candidates. Eventually, 51 percent of the Black candidates ultimately passed the CONNCEPT (which may be taken as often as a candidate wishes), compared with 82 percent of White candidates.[63] This pattern indicates that remediation and persistence pay off for both Black candidates and White candidates. But roughly half of the Black candidates continue to fail the CONNCEPT after multiple attempts, and consequently are either denied entry to undergraduate teacher training programs or, for out-of-state candidates, are ineligible for the initial license needed to teach in Connecticut.

Once again we see that the use of standardized tests to screen applicants for teaching licenses restricts the number of Black students who become teachers. This emphasizes the importance of developing strategies for attracting academically strong members of minority groups into teaching. The New Jersey experience suggests that targeted financial inducements and the creation of alternatives to undergraduate teacher training may help achieve this goal.[64]

Reforming Licensing Requirements: Necessary, But Not Enough

We have argued that although traditional teacher licensing regulations are deeply flawed—they deter many talented college graduates from entering teaching, and they provide no incentives for the development of high-quality teacher training—the appropriate response is not to eliminate licensing. Eliminating licensing would further weaken the quality of the teaching force in communities where, as a result of inadequate financing, patronage, skewed priorities, or poor personnel practices, effective teachers are not recruited and hired. The challenge is to develop licensing procedures that reduce the likelihood that local districts will hire incompetent teachers, to promote the development of high-quality teacher training, and to not deter the most able college students from trying teaching.

Much remains to be learned about how to design and administer performance-based assessments. But recent developments are promising, and a long-term plan of basing licensing on well-conceived, carefully administered assessments of teaching performance should be one element of a strategy for staffing the schools with skilled teachers.

Reforming licensing requirements cannot be the only element of this strategy, however. The reason is simple: raising the standards for entry will improve the teaching force only if talented college graduates with many occupational alternatives find teaching attractive. In Chapter 8 we discuss strategies that contribute to this end.

8

Getting the Incentives Right

American elementary and secondary education needs improvement. Recognizing that improvement depends critically on staffing the schools with increased numbers of thoughtful, skilled, and motivated teachers, local school boards and state legislators have enacted a number of policies designed to raise standards. What has sometimes been forgotten is that legislators and school boards cannot mandate improvements in the nation's teaching force. How policies affect the quality of education provided to students depends on the responses of the teachers themselves.

We have described how teachers, prospective teachers, and former teachers respond to the incentives they face, and we have seen that their career decisions—whether to enter teaching, how long to stay in teaching, and whether to return to teaching after a career interruption—are extremely sensitive to incentives. The key to policy design is to "get the incentives right."

Fruitless Policies

Mandatory master's degrees, supplemental pay for master's degrees, and merit pay are fruitless policies that fail to improve teaching. They raise the cost of becoming a teacher and the cost of employing teachers without commensurate benefits.

The mandatory master's degree

Several states, including California and New York, require that teachers earn a master's degree within a specified period of time after initial hiring.[1] Teachers who do not comply lose their positions. The Holmes Group, an organization of leading schools of education, proposes that all candidates for a teaching license earn a master's degree *before* they start teaching.

Mandating master's degrees will not help to staff the schools with skilled teachers. What such a policy does do is raise the cost of becoming a teacher. Prospective teachers must not only pay for an additional year's tuition but, under the Holmes Group proposal, must also forgo a year's salary. Together, these costs total $20,000 to $30,000, a burden likely to deter many talented college graduates from trying teaching.

These costs might be justified, of course, if a mandatory master's degree dramatically improved teachers' effectiveness. But the evidence is quite the opposite. In a comprehensive review, Eric Hanushek examined 106 studies that compared the effectiveness (usually measured by students' test-score gains) of teachers with master's degrees and those who held only bachelor's degrees. Of these studies, 95 studies showed no difference in effectiveness; 6 showed that teachers with master's degrees were more effective, on average; and 5 found that teachers without master's degrees were more effective.[2]

The Holmes Group might respond by arguing that the clinical master's degree programs it envisions would offer more effective training than traditional master's degree programs have provided. Although we agree that participation in a clinical master's program of high quality can enhance prospective teachers' skills, this is not sufficient justification for a master's degree requirement. As discussed in Chapter 7, prospective teachers can acquire critical skills in a variety of ways. Because many of the alternatives impose fewer costs on prospective teachers than a full-time year of postgraduate study, they are likely to attract more talented college graduates into teaching.

Mandatory master's degrees also create the wrong incentives for training institutions. Even the Holmes Group proposal would stifle innovation. Implementation would lead to a list of specifications that graduate programs must satisfy in order to have their graduates eligible for licensure. Administrators of schools of education would design programs with two goals in mind: first, meeting the specifications, and second, making the program sufficiently convenient in order to attract students. Concern with these goals would overwhelm what should be the primary concern: designing a creative program that enhances participants' skills.

Paying for master's degrees

Virtually all of the nation's fifteen thousand school districts provide salary premiums for teachers who hold master's degrees. The premiums range from a few hundred dollars to a few thousand dollars. Paying teachers with master's degrees more than teachers who hold only bachelor's degrees is a poor use of scarce school resources. Again, the reasons concern incentives. The pay premium provides strong incentives for teachers to earn master's degrees. Teachers respond to these incentives. In 1986, 51 percent of the teaching force held master's degrees.[3] These responses have translated into high costs to local school districts. Because the salary premium a teacher receives for earning a master's degree does not hinge on a demonstration of enhanced skills, teachers have a strong incentive to find a program that does not unduly tax their busy lives. Schools of education, which depend heavily on tuition dollars, have strong incentives to respond to prospective students' wishes and offer convenient and undemanding programs. These factors may explain Hanushek's finding that teachers with master's degrees are no more effective than teachers who hold only bachelor's degrees.

We do not propose that local school districts eliminate the master's degree premium for current teachers. Such action would violate collectively bargained contracts between teachers' unions and districts. It would also have disastrous effects on morale, especially for those teachers who had earned master's degrees with the understanding that they would receive higher pay. Instead, future contracts should eliminate the master's degree pay premium for newly hired teachers.

Why do we recommend this radical change? Because the costs of this practice are unwarranted, given the lack of evidence of its benefits. But our goal is not to reduce teachers' compensation. Salary increases are essential for recruiting more able teachers into the nation's schools, as we shall argue later in this chapter. Nor do we believe that training cannot improve teachers' performance. Finding ways to encourage training institutions to provide high-quality educational experiences and finding ways to encourage teachers to invest their energies in learning to become better teachers are essential. But mandatory master's degrees and pay premiums for holding this degree are ineffective tools. They create the wrong incentives for teachers and for training institutions.

Merit pay

A third fruitless policy is merit pay for individual teachers. This observation may seem surprising initially. After all, teachers do vary in effectiveness. Shouldn't we reward excellence and pay the more effective teachers more?

Merit pay is an old idea, dating back to the turn of the century in the United States. Almost all merit pay plans are short-lived, typically lasting only three to four years. Union resistance is not to blame. Merit pay plans have a history of failure that includes trials in many districts without teachers' unions. Most plans fail because they hurt morale and are costly to administer. Even teachers picked by their peers as worthy recipients of merit pay because of their superior teaching oppose the idea.[4] Although literally thousands of American school districts have tried merit pay over the last ninety years, there is not a single case documenting that it helped improve a troubled school district's performance.

To explore why merit pay, which seems so promising, has fared so poorly, David Cohen and Richard Murnane looked for counterexamples, districts that had used merit pay for an extended period of time, and where the merit pay bonuses were large enough (at least $600) to influence teachers' behavior. After considerable search, they located six districts that met these criteria. They conducted field research in each district, interviewing teachers and administrators to try to understand how merit pay worked, why it had survived, and what it accomplished.[5]

In every case, merit pay was added to a uniform salary scale that was already competitive with the best salaries offered by other districts in the vicinity. These six districts had long histories of offering high-quality education, primarily to students from middle-class families, and the reputation for high quality antedated the introduction of merit pay. But most important, these were not conventional merit pay programs. Instead, they had one or more of the following characteristics:

- *Extra pay for extra work.* The criteria determining who was awarded extra pay emphasized extra duties outside the classroom, and deemphasized classroom performance.

- *Everyone wins.* In one district, teachers received awards of $500, $1,000, $1,500, or $2,000. Although it was a matter of considerable secrecy who received merit pay and how much individual teachers received, the plan's popularity stemmed from the fact that every participating teacher (over 90 percent of teachers in the district) received merit pay, and that 85 percent received either $1,500 or $2,000.

- *Make merit pay inconspicuous.* In several districts, the merit pay plans were of little interest to most teachers because participation required too much extra work. For example, to receive the maximum award of $4,000 in one district, a teacher not only had to acquire a master's degree plus thirty hours of graduate credits but also had to serve on a state or national committee and be an officer in a professional organization.

Cohen and Murnane found that most merit pay plans died because administrators could not provide convincing answers to two questions from teachers: Why did my colleague get merit pay, and I did not? and What can I do to get merit pay? In the districts where merit pay lasted, the answer to the first question was that the colleague had run the Book Fair, the French Club, and had directed the school play. The answer to the second question was that other teachers could get merit pay by doing similar work. In districts in which the "everyone wins" policy was in effect, of course, few teachers asked either of these questions.

Merit pay continues to be proposed as a strategy for improving the quality of teaching in American schools. No other reform has been tried so often. But for no other reform is the evidence so clear: merit pay for individual teachers does not improve the quality of teaching in a troubled school district.

Elements of a Promising Strategy

How can we get the incentives right? As we argue in Chapter 7, one crucial change is to replace mandatory training requirements with assessments of whether candidates for teaching licenses can do the work of teaching. Overhauling licensing requirements is essential to achieving the dual goals of raising the minimum performance standards college graduates must meet to teach in the nation's schools and increasing the supply of new teachers. But performance-based licensing will result in better teaching in the nation's schools only if the applicant pool is strong. For this reason, we propose a number of policies for attracting talented college graduates to teaching.

Higher salaries

As discussed in Chapter 3, we know that the competitiveness of teaching salaries with salaries in occupational alternatives affects the supply of college graduates who choose to enter teaching.[6] We also know that teaching salaries affect the length of time that teachers remain in the profession, as described in Chapter 5. Teachers who were paid $2,000 per year above the state average in Michigan and North Carolina were about half as likely to leave teaching after only one year than were teachers paid $2,000 below the state average. These differences accumulated over time so that a $2,000 annual salary differential corresponded to a difference in median employment duration of one to two years. Salaries do affect who teaches in the nation's schools.

How high must salaries be to attract a strong applicant pool and to keep teachers in the classroom for at least the four or five years that it takes them to make a significant contribution? Here, the evidence is not clear. Simply comparing teaching salaries with those in other professions is not helpful, because the work differs. Teachers typically have specific duties for only ten months of the year, compared with eleven months in other professions. Yet, for many teachers, the school year is stressful and absorbs a great many hours per week. The important question is not whether teaching salaries are equal to those in other professions, but whether they are high enough to attract a strong pool of applicants. One way to judge the adequacy of teachers' salaries is to examine whether the teaching profession is attracting a pool of applicants whose cognitive abilities are at least as high, on average, as the average ability of the nation's college graduates. As several of the reports on education of the 1980s emphasized, this has not been the case in recent years.

Should salary increases be equally distributed among teachers with different levels of experience? We cannot answer this question definitively, because we do not know how the structure of salary schedules influences the career decisions of prospective teachers. For two reasons, however, there is a particular need for increases in the salaries of beginning teachers. First, beginning teachers' salaries fell more (in constant purchasing power terms) than did the salaries of experienced teachers during the inflationary period of the late 1970s and early 1980s.[7] In these years the politics of collective bargaining produced larger salary increases for experienced teachers than for novice teachers. For example, between 1970 and 1980 the average constant dollar salary of beginning Michigan teachers fell by 20 percent, while the average salary of teachers with fifteen years of experience fell by only 15 percent.[8]

Second, salaries affect the career decisions of beginning teachers more than the career decisions of experienced teachers. Relatively high starting salaries would reduce the number of districts that find themselves on treadmills, repeatedly hiring new, inexperienced teachers to replace teachers who leave after one or two years. It is important to retain novice teachers. Studies have shown that teachers make marked gains in effectiveness during their first years in the classroom.[9] Reducing the frequency with which children are taught by a successive stream of beginning teachers is one step toward improving educational quality.

Flexibility in salaries for teachers in shortage fields

As we discussed in Chapter 1, Joseph Kershaw and Roland McKean argued in the early 1960s that the use of uniform salary schedules, which base pay solely on seniority and degrees, makes it extremely difficult for school districts to attract and retain teachers in areas such as chemistry and physics that are in high demand in other sectors of the economy. In Chapters 5 and 6 we presented evidence supporting Kershaw and McKean's argument. Chemistry and physics teachers tend to have extremely short careers in teaching. Moreover, they are much less likely than teachers of other subjects to return to the classroom after a career interruption.

We support Kershaw and McKean's proposed remedy to the shortage problem, which is to pay salary premiums to teachers *in shortage fields*. Such a practice must be distinguished from merit pay. Merit pay, as we define it, refers to differences in salary related to management's perception that different teachers are doing the *same job differentially well*.

Conventional wisdom is that pay differentials based on subject field are politically untenable because they violate the principle of the uniform salary scale. Our field work reveals, however, that variants of Kershaw and McKean's proposal are not uncommon. The Grandview school district described in Chapter 4, for example, convinces particularly strong applicants in mathematics and science to accept teaching positions by placing them several steps higher on the salary scale than where they would otherwise begin. Even the Harteville school district, also described in Chapter 4, has its variant of specially treating applicants in shortage areas. Operating under severe financial constraints, this district typically hires new teachers as permanent substitutes rather than as regular teachers (at an annual savings of approximately $9,000 per teacher). But the district tries to attract applicants in mathematics, chemistry, and physics by offering them regular contracts.

A number of recent collectively bargained teachers' contracts explicitly permit flexibility in salary determination. For example, the 1990–1992 Boston teachers' contract states: "For the purposes of recruiting teachers into areas where there may be a teacher shortage . . . , the [School] Committee may place newly hired teachers on any step of the salary grid."[10] Contracts in many other districts, including Hartford, Connecticut, and Detroit, Michigan, have similar provisions.[11] The following section from an educational reform report adopted by the American Federation of Teachers (AFT) in 1986 suggests that this practice may become more widespread: "As an incentive to attracting and hiring teachers in all areas of shortages, as they develop, the AFT recommends that [union] locals and school districts consider placing entering teachers in areas of shortage on higher steps of the salary schedule."[12] These examples suggest that teachers' unions and local school district managers can negotiate contract provisions that increase flexibility in hiring practices. There is no single right way to do this, and the extent of flexibility and the method of achieving it will vary from district to district. But the essential point is that flexibility in salary determination is one potentially fruitful strategy for attracting strong teachers in all subject areas to the schools.

Better working conditions

Pay is not the only aspect of the job that influences teachers' and prospective teachers' career decisions. As Susan Johnson explains in her recent book, *Teachers at Work,* many talented teachers leave teaching because their school environments do not support the adaptability, individuality, and autonomy needed to teach effectively. Making schools better workplaces is critical to attracting and retaining skilled teachers.[13] We do not build this case in detail because the argument rests on a type of research very different from that underlying this book. Johnson's book, moreover, makes the case convincingly.

One area of special need should be mentioned, however: support for beginning teachers. Our research, as well as earlier studies, documents that teachers are most likely to leave teaching during or after their first year in the classroom. Many beginning teachers resign before they learn how to deal with the demands of their difficult jobs. Learning to cope with the stresses of teaching is particularly difficult for teachers in large cities, where the proportion of children from poor families and the proportion with special needs are higher than in suburban communities. This helps to explain why, as discussed in Chapter 5, teachers who start their careers in big city schools are less likely to teach for at least five years than are teachers who begin their careers in suburban schools.

Helping beginning teachers, particularly those working in large cities, to learn to cope with the demands of their students is a critical challenge facing the schools. Many strategies are possible, including providing each novice teacher with a mentor and reducing the student load for beginning teachers. There are no recipes. Each district will need to devise its own strategy.

Supporting the efforts of beginning teachers who have the capabilities to be good teachers if they can overcome initial problems would reduce the number of children who are taught by a series of novices. It might also increase the number of Black teachers in the nation's schools, given that Black teachers are particularly likely to work in big-city schools, where resignation rates of novice teachers are particularly high.

Better recruiting, screening, and hiring practices

Attractive salaries and good working conditions alone will not guarantee a skilled teaching force. Recruiting practices must yield a large pool of applicants, screening practices must identify strong candidates, and hiring practices must secure commitments from the chosen candidates. In Chapter 4 we reviewed the extent to which recruiting, screening, and hiring practices vary across districts, and noted that some districts' practices are so deficient that salary increases may not result in a stronger teaching staff.

There is no one path to reforming personnel practices. The sources of the problems vary from district to district. Some districts' problems stem from inadequate finances, which prevent making timely offers to strong candidates. Other districts' problems stem from poor management practices. Just as the sources of the problems vary, so must the strategies for improving practices.

There are, however, a number of relatively simple checks that a district can use to assess how well its personnel practices are working. District administrators should ask: How many applicants are there per vacancy in each subject field and grade level? Do the principal and the staff of the school with a vacancy help decide who will fill the vacancy? What proportion of the candidates offered jobs accept the positions? The answers to these questions provide a crude sense of how well the district's personnel practices are operating, and may help to identify problem

areas. Changes over time in the answers to the questions provide bench-
marks to use in judging whether personnel practices are improving.

Support for initiative

We believe that teachers who will most effectively help our children
learn are those adults who want to continue to learn themselves, and to
experiment with new ideas and new ways of teaching. In order to attract
teachers with these priorities, the public schools must support learning
and experimentation. There are many ways to do this; here we suggest
two simple approaches.

The first is that school districts pay the tuition for courses teachers
would like to take during the evening or during the summer. Districts
should also offer small stipends to cover out-of-pocket costs for books,
transportation, and childcare to encourage teachers to engage in learning
experiences. This expense reimbursement should be provided for courses
that are even remotely related to a teacher's work. Teachers will continue
to be effective as teachers only if they continue to be learners. It is up to
districts to promote learning.

This tuition policy would change the incentives teachers and training
institutions face. Under current practice, when master's degrees are either
required or result in substantial salary premiums, teachers have incentives to shop for the program that makes the fewest demands on their
busy lives. Training institutions, anxious for large enrollments, have incentives to offer programs with the same characteristics. Under our policy, teachers have incentives to shop for courses they find interesting and
useful, and training institutions have the incentive to meet this demand.

Our second proposal is that districts offer small grants, ranging, say,
from several hundred dollars to one thousand dollars, to teachers for
innovative projects. These projects might include the design of new curricula, carrying out a class project with students, or any other idea related
in some way to classroom instruction. Teachers would write short proposals describing their projects and presenting their budgets. A committee, consisting perhaps of teachers, administrators, and parents, would
read the proposals and rate them. Recipients of grants would be required
to write a brief report at the end of the grant period describing how they
had used the grant money and what they felt they had accomplished. This
idea of small grants for innovative projects has been tried in a number of
settings and has an attractive track record. One evaluation found that it

had an important positive impact on teacher morale and led to a variety of interesting projects.[14]

Stimulating Change

We have made a number of recommendations for policy changes that we believe will help the nation's public schools to attract and retain skilled, energetic teachers. But readers may ask: If these policies are such good ideas, why aren't they already in place? Our answer has two parts.

Many of these proposals *are* operating with considerable success in particular school districts. Many districts have small grant programs. Other districts offer salary premiums to strong candidates for teaching positions in shortage fields. Moreover, the growing concern about the quality of American public education is putting current practices under close scrutiny and producing a greater willingness to try out new ones. The growing number of states with "alternative route" programs for obtaining a teaching license is an example of a creative policy response.

But many school districts are locked into weak management practices, including ineffective recruiting, screening, and hiring practices. In some districts, a history of antagonistic relationships between school district managers and teachers' unions is a crucial part of the explanation. In others, the overwhelming weight of bureaucracy makes change difficult, particularly in large cities. In still others, education is held hostage to local politics, and teachers are hired on the basis of political connections, not teaching skills.

There is no single remedy for the poor management practices of many school districts. Problems differ, and so must remedies. In some districts, major shifts in governance structure will be necessary to bring about meaningful change. Proposals for accomplishing this abound, and include increasing family choice and school based management. Our proposals do not compete with proposals to alter the balance of power in local school districts. In fact, they are complementary. Organizational change may create the political will to break away from ineffective management practices that hinder districts from effectively recruiting skilled teachers. If this occurs, policies recommended here will help attract and retain skilled teachers. More important, in debates about the details of family choice plans or school-based management plans, it is critical to ask: How would teachers respond to the incentives implicit in the plan? Do the details of the plan make teaching a more attractive occupation for skilled, energetic college graduates? Rarely have debates about family choice and school-based management even mentioned this critical perspective.

Critical Questions

We began with four questions that are crucial to the well-being of American schools: (1) Do dollars make a difference? (2) Can we find enough mathematics and science teachers? (3) Are we losing the brightest? (4) Why are there fewer and fewer Black teachers? Evidence on teachers' career patterns has shed light on the answers to these questions. Let us now return to these questions, review the evidence, and examine how our policy proposals inform the answers.

Do dollars make a difference?

We have summarized the results of studies showing that the competitiveness of teaching salaries influences the occupational decisions of college students. We have also shown that salaries influence how long teachers remain in the classroom. Finally, we have shown that inadequate funding levels contribute to ineffective personnel practices in some school districts. Thus a necessary condition for effective schooling is a funding level adequate to attract a strong pool of applicants for teaching positions, to hire the best candidates, and to maintain working conditions that talented teachers with good options in other fields find attractive.

At the same time, a high level of funding is not a sufficient condition for effective schooling. In too many cases, resources have not been used wisely. Examples include ineffective personnel practices, and pay premiums for master's degrees. Such policies do not contribute either to attracting or retaining skilled teachers. A basic lesson here is the importance both of providing schools with the resources needed to attract and retain skilled teachers and of examining whether the dollars are used in a manner that promotes these goals.

Can we find enough mathematics and science teachers?

We have shown that teachers of particular subjects, most notably chemistry and physics, tend to have very short teaching careers, and are particularly unlikely to return to teaching after career interruptions. These findings are consistent with Kershaw and McKean's hypothesis that the schools have difficulty attracting and retaining teachers whose subject specialties command high salaries in business and industry. Because of this, we recommend more flexibility in salary determination.

Our findings also indicate that it is a mistake to treat mathematics and science as a homogeneous shortage area. Biology teachers typically do not have short teaching careers, a pattern consistent with Kershaw and McKean's perspective because biology majors earn considerably less in business and industry than do chemistry and physics majors. We also found that mathematics teachers tend to stay in teaching longer than do chemistry and physics teachers—an unexpected pattern, because starting salaries in business and industry are about as high for mathematics majors as for chemistry and physics majors. Evidence from Connecticut showing that a much lower percentage of mathematics teachers majored in their teaching specialty than was the case for chemistry and physics teachers suggests an explanation. Many mathematics teachers are unable to obtain the high salaries offered by business and industry to mathematics majors.

Our findings show that the designation "mathematics and science" is not synonymous with "shortage area." The subject fields that constitute shortage areas will fluctuate over time and from region to region. They will also be influenced by changes in the demand for college graduates in different fields. A decline in defense spending, for example, may reduce the demand for college graduates majoring in physics, with an ensuing increase in the supply of physics teachers. It would be a mistake to negotiate contracts under which mathematics and science teachers as a group are paid more than other teachers. Instead, negotiated settlements should provide school districts with the flexibility to offer higher salaries to strong candidates in those fields in which it proves difficult to find qualified job candidates.

Are we losing the brightest?

In the late 1960s, academically talented college graduates were almost as likely to enter teaching as were college graduates of average ability. Over the next fourteen years, the pattern changed. By 1980 a college graduate with an IQ of 130 was only one fourth as likely to become a teacher as was a college graduate with an IQ of 100. The most academically talented teachers were particularly likely to have very short teaching careers and were especially unlikely to return to teaching after a career interruption.

Thus, increasingly, the public schools *are* losing the brightest college graduates. In an important respect this was to be expected, as the civil rights and feminist movements opened opportunities in other sectors of the economy for minorities and women. As a result of these new opportunities, the groups that were the most likely to enter teaching in the past now have a wider range of options, and public education must compete for talent in ways that it did not in the past.

We have suggested several policies that will help the schools attract more of the nation's most academically able college graduates. One is competitive salaries. A second is support for continued learning and experimentation. A third is a change in licensing requirements to eliminate compulsory undergraduate teacher training, and replace it with demonstration of teaching skills. There is abundant evidence—from our quantitative studies, from New Jersey's Provisional Teacher Program, and from evaluations of small grant programs—that these policies will attract more talented college graduates to the nation's schools.

Why are there fewer and fewer Black teachers?

As we explain in Chapter 1, not only the decline in the percentage of Black teachers but also the underrepresentation of Hispanics and other minorities in the teaching force presents a serious policy problem. Unfortunately, there are almost no data available on the career paths of Hispanic teachers or teachers in other minority groups. Consequently, in our study of minority group representation in the teaching force, we were able to focus only on Black teachers.

At least four sets of factors have contributed to the decline in the proportion of Black college graduates in the nation's teaching force. The first is the poverty in which a large proportion of the nation's Black children live, and the poor quality of the elementary and secondary education they receive. As a result of these handicaps, the proportion of Black students who graduate from high school and complete college, thus achieving the minimum credentials to teach, is lower than the proportion of White students who graduate from college.

Second, Black college students have been deterred by the increasingly common requirement that applicants for teaching licenses score above specified levels on standardized tests, especially the NTE tests. Black college students are more likely than White students to score below the cutoffs and hence to be denied teaching licenses. Black students are aware of this potential career hurdle, and many choose to prepare for other occupations.

Third, opportunities for Black college graduates outside of education have improved. Teaching provided the only professional employment opportunity for many Black female college graduates twenty years ago, but this is no longer the case. Among Black women graduating from college during the period 1980–1984, 62 percent found jobs in professional occupations other than teaching; the comparable figure for Black women graduating in the early 1970s is 31 percent.[15]

Fourth, Black teachers are much more likely than White teachers to start their teaching careers in urban schools, where the resignation rate for beginning teachers is especially high.

We have found consistent evidence that Black and White college graduates' career decisions are equally sensitive to incentives, and therefore several of our policy recommendations will make teaching more attractive to Black college graduates. First, our proposals to attract more of the most academically able college graduates into teaching—through higher salaries and more support for continued learning and experimentation—should be as compelling to talented Black college graduates as to White graduates. Second, our proposal to eliminate mandatory teacher education requirements should dramatically increase the number of talented Black college graduates who enter teaching. Recall that 21 percent of the participants in the New Jersey Provisional Teacher Program have been minority group members, who, like other participants, satisfied the NTE test-score requirement.

An unanswered question is whether our recommendation that licensing requirements include assessments of candidates' teaching skills will deter Black college graduates from entering teaching. We view this assessment as a critical complement to the elimination of training requirements. It is the state's only means of ensuring that some local school districts will not hire unskilled adults to serve as teachers. As yet, there is no track record concerning the passing rates of Black candidates on performance assessments that are part of licensing procedures. Evidence from other occupations, however, indicates that minority group members do better on performance-based assessments than they do on pencil-and-paper tests.[16]

We believe that the goal of achieving high standards for obtaining a teaching license is compatible with the goal of attracting more Black college graduates into the teaching profession. One part of the strategy for achieving these two goals is to ensure that the "standards" do, in fact, reflect skills needed to teach effectively. A second part is to make teaching attractive to talented Black college graduates who have other good career options.

A Final Word

At the root of all of the policies recommended in this chapter is a common theme: Get the incentives right. This is not easy to accomplish. It often takes considerable experimentation to learn how teachers and prospective teachers will respond to particular policies. Frequently there are political obstacles to altering policies that influence who can teach, how candidates are recruited and screened, and how teachers are compensated. Negotiation, patience, and persistence will be needed to design and implement policies that will attract skilled teachers to the classroom, and provide them with reasons to stay in teaching. The critical lesson of this book is that there is no alternative to getting the incentives right. This must be at the center of any successful strategy for staffing the nation's schools with skilled teachers. It is this lesson that we hope every reader will take from our book.

Appendixes
Notes
Index

Appendix A

Research Context: Whom Did We Study?

Because there were no easily accessible state and national teacher career path data readily available to us, we began our investigation by assembling several large databases appropriate for our analyses. These databases contain data on the career paths of teachers at both the state and the national level.

Our state databases contain the career histories of the thousands of men and women who were certified to teach or who began to teach in either North Carolina or Michigan in the 1970s, and who had never taught before. The databases are very rich, containing information on the characteristics of the teachers, their job assignments, and their school districts. Unfortunately, the state databases contain no information on the employment histories of individuals *outside* of teaching. We do not know what jobs were taken by those who left teaching for other fields. Nor do we know the previous employment histories of new entrants into teaching or of former teachers who reenter the classroom later in their careers. To fill in these gaps, we complemented our state databases with data obtained at the national level by the National Longitudinal Surveys of Labor Market Experience (NLS). Brief details of the two state databases and the national database follow.

The State Databases.[1] These data were obtained directly from the North Carolina and Michigan Departments of Education themselves and contain information on the demographic characteristics, education, subject-matter specialty, career status, salary, and entering school district for all individuals. In North Carolina, scores on the NTE were also available. The Michigan database contains the employment histories of the 30,614 individuals who entered teaching in the Michigan public schools between September 1972 and September 1981 and who were followed through the 1984–85 school year. The North Carolina database contains information on the career paths of the 50,502 individuals who were licensed by North Carolina for employment in public education between January 1974 and

December 1985 and who were followed through the 1985–86 school year. In both states, only those individuals with no prior teaching experience were included and, in addition, nonclassroom education personnel (such as administrators and guidance counselors) were excluded. The databases contain only those teachers whose race was classified as either "Black" or "White;" omitted, for reasons explained in Chapter 1, were 250 teachers in Michigan and 400 teachers in North Carolina whose race was classified by the states as "other."

The NLS Database.[2] Our NLS database is derived from three nationally representative longitudinal surveys (the NLS surveys of "Young Men," "Young Women" and "Youth") and contains information on individual characteristics, education, employment, and teaching status. We obtained the NLS survey data from the Center for Human Resource Research at Ohio State University. Our database includes information on the histories of the 2,539 sampled individuals who graduated from college between 1967 and 1985. In all three surveys, young people were between the ages of 14 and 24 when first interviewed. The "Young Men" were first interviewed in 1966 and they were subsequently surveyed yearly from 1967 through 1971, and also in 1973, 1975, 1976, 1978, 1980, and 1981. The "Young Women" were first interviewed in 1968 and were subsequently surveyed yearly from 1969 through 1973, and also in 1975, 1977, 1978, 1980, 1982, 1983, and 1985. The "Youth" were interviewed yearly from 1979 through 1987. Our database contains only those young people whose race was originally classified as "Black" or "White," for consistency with the state databases.

The fact that Michigan and North Carolina differ both geographically and economically, allowed us to evaluate the effect of context on teacher career patterns. In Table A.1, we contrast selected economic, social, and educational characteristics of Michigan, North Carolina, and the nation as a whole using 1980 as a base year. In 1980 both states were among the most populous in the nation, but in Michigan there were almost twice as many public schools as in North Carolina, and students were distributed over more than four times as many school districts. College graduation rates were approximately equal in the two states, but the high school graduation rate in North Carolina was 11 points lower than the national average.

   The fraction of the general population and the public school student population that belonged to minority groups differed considerably in Michigan and North Carolina. Hispanic Americans were underrepresented in both states. Black Americans had a much larger presence in North Carolina than might be expected on the basis of nationwide figures. And, as is true for the nation as a whole, these proportions sit in stark contrast to the composition of the teacher work force. In 1981, in public schools in both states, the proportion of teachers who were White was 10 percent higher than the proportion of students who were White.[3]

   In 1980, per capita income in Michigan was considerably higher than in North Carolina and per pupil expenditures on education mirrored these differences in

Table A.1   Educational and economic characteristics of Michigan, North Carolina, and the nation as a whole in 1980 and for the 1980–81 school year.

Characteristics	Michigan	North Carolina	Nationwide
Population (millions)	9.3	5.9	226.5
Percentage of population			
Black	12.9	22.4	11.7
Hispanic	1.8	1.0	6.4
White	85.0	76.0	83.1
Percentage of adults completing			
4 years of high school	68.2	55.3	66.3
4 years of college	15.2	13.4	16.3
Number of school districts	575	144	15,912
Number of public schools	3,688	2,001	83,688
Elementary	2,748	1,403	59,326
Secondary	895	550	22,619
Combined elem./sec.	45	48	1,743
Number of public school teachers	84,377	56,222	2,183,538
Percentage of school-aged children in public school	89.0	95.0	87.0
Public school enrollment	1,519,742	1,123,840	40,989,000
Percentage of public school enrollment			
Black	17.9	29.6	16.1
Hispanic	1.8	0.2	8.0
White	78.7	68.1	73.3
Per capita income[a]	$9,798	$7,774	$9,494
Per pupil expenditure[a]	$2,874	$2,149	$2,637

Sources: Population and income statistics from U.S. Bureau of the Census, *State and Metropolitan Area Data Book, 1986* (Washington, D.C.: U.S. Government Printing Office, 1986), and U.S. Bureau of the Census, *Statistical Abstract of the United States, 1989* (Washington, D.C.: U.S. Government Printing Office, 1989). School-based statistics from *Digest of Education Statistics* (Washington, D.C.: Center for Education Statistics, 1982 and 1983–84 editions).

[a] In 1980 dollars.

income. Surprisingly, though, the average starting salaries paid to teachers in the two states were about the same and approximately one-fifth higher than the national average. In Michigan, a new teacher with a bachelor's degree and no prior teaching experience was paid $12,984 (in 1980 dollars); in North Carolina, starting salary averaged $12,616.[4] The range of starting salaries was smaller in North Carolina than in Michigan, however, because the state government in North Carolina specified a minimum statewide teacher salary scale and provided school districts with funds to pay teachers according to this scale. In addition,

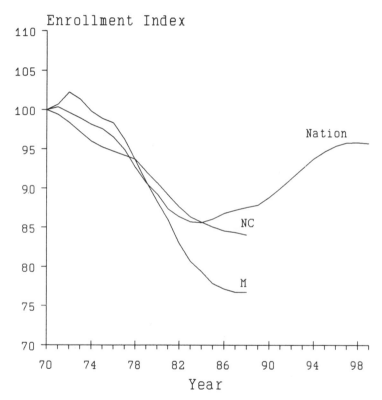

Figure A.1 Enrollment trends for North Carolina (NC), Michigan (M), and the nation. (State enrollment numbers provided by the Michigan State Department of Education and the Comptroller's Office for the North Carolina State Board of Education. National enrollment numbers obtained from the National Center for Education Statistics, *Projections of Education Statistics to 2000,* Washington, D.C.: U.S. Department of Education, 1989. Enrollment index based on setting the 1970 enrollment figures equal to 100.)

approximately half the school districts supplemented the state-specified minimum salary.

Michigan and North Carolina are interesting examples of the social and economic conditions that prevailed in many of the larger states during the 1970s and 1980s. Michigan is a midwestern manufacturing state with several densely populated urban centers. Like most of the "rust belt" states, it suffered during the economic crises of the early 1970s and faced massive enrollment declines in the public schools as its unemployed work force migrated elsewhere. North Carolina, by contrast, is a southern state with a considerable proportion of its school population scattered throughout rural and mountainous areas. Like many of the "sun belt" states, it suffered less during the economic crises in the early seventies, and school enrollment declines were delayed and less dramatic. These enrollment trends are summarized in Figure A.1.

Not all the data that are included in our databases were analyzed to answer each of our research questions (for details, see Appendix B). In order to make predictions about the teacher career patterns that are likely to prevail in the 1990s, we examined the time period in our databases that most closely resembled the coming years. Elementary and secondary school student enrollments, the primary driving force behind the demand for teachers, are projected to increase or at least remain stable during the 1990s. As can be seen in Figure A.1, for North Carolina, Michigan, and the nation as a whole this was last true in the early to mid-1970s. Consequently, in our analyses, we focused on teachers who began their careers in this period. Finally, by examining teachers who began their careers when enrollments were relatively stable, we were able to minimize the possibility that these teachers were involuntarily transferred or laid off[5] and consequently base our inferences on the assumption that teacher career changes were voluntary.[6]

Despite the important economic, social, and educational differences between North Carolina and Michigan, teacher career paths in the two states are remarkably similar. In addition, the patterns we have identified in the national database strongly support the findings from the states. This striking consonance of findings, across widely disparate data sources and obtained for the last time period in which student enrollments were relatively stable, form a stalwart basis for our assertion that the teacher career patterns we have identified are also likely to prevail in the coming years.

Appendix B

Methodology

We have used a variety of statistical techniques to answer our research questions. Throughout the book, descriptive statistics, cross-tabulations, and plots are used to display and summarize raw trends in frequencies and percentages. In Chapter 3, logistic regression analysis allows the relationship between "entry into teaching," a dichotomous outcome, and characteristics of college graduates to be investigated. In Chapters 5 and 6, survival analysis is used to examine the relationship between measures of duration, such as the length of the teaching career and the length of time spent out of teaching before returning, and background characteristics of the teachers and their school districts.

In Chapters 1–8 we present our findings and their implications for education in the coming years. In the three sections of this appendix, corresponding to Chapters 3, 5, and 6, we outline our principal analytic strategies and present an overview of the fitted statistical models on which our findings are based. Further details of the analyses can be obtained directly from the authors.

Statistical Analyses: Chapter 3

In Chapter 3, we examine the relationship between "entry into teaching" (whether a qualified college graduate entered the teaching profession within some prespecified time after becoming qualified) and the demographic characteristics and qualifications of the graduate. The chapter has two sections, one describing national trends in the decision to enter teaching, the other focusing on entry into teaching in North Carolina.

In the first section, we use data from the National Longitudinal Surveys (NLS) of Young Men, Young Women, and Youth (our "national database") to describe the characteristics of college students who graduated from college between 1967 and 1984 and who entered teaching (public and private, elementary and secondary) within five years of graduation. Multiple logistic regression analysis was used to model the relationship between the dichotomous outcome ("entry into teaching within five years of graduation" versus "no entry within five years of graduation") and several predictors: graduation year, race, gender, age at graduation, college major, and standardized test score (Table B.1).[1] We included in our logit analyses only those students who graduated between 1967 and 1984, and we restricted the potential period for entry into teaching to five years after graduation so that all students had a period of identical length within which to become teachers.

Our approach was to build up a hierarchy of multiple logistic regression models in which predictors were added systematically and the effects of potential two-way and higher-order interactions among the predictors evaluated. Table B.2 presents a selected array of the final fitted models from which our principal findings derive. The initial model included only graduation year as a predictor (Model 3.1). Subsequent models added predictors that described immutable characteristics of the graduate: race (Model 3.2) and gender (Model 3.3). Finally, predictors that described the academic record of the graduates were added: age at graduation and college major (Model 3.4), and standardized test score (Models 3.5 and 3.6).

In Table B.2, and all other tables of fitted models in this Appendix, the overall goodness-of-fit of each statistical model is described by a pair of summary statistics. The *baseline chi-square statistic* describes the goodness-of-fit of a logistic regression model in which only the intercept is included as a predictor. The *change in the chi-square statistic* indicates the decrement in the baseline chi-square statistic on addition of the listed predictors. This latter statistic, in conjunction with the number of predictors added, permits testing of the null hypothesis that goodness-of-fit is not improved by the addition of all the listed predictors simultaneously. In addition, appended as a superscript to individual parameter estimates is an approximate *p*-value suitable for testing the null hypothesis that goodness-of-fit is not improved by adding that single predictor last. This pair of statistical tests permits evaluation of the statistical significance of our findings.

To display key findings derived from the fitted models, in Chapter 3 and throughout the book, fitted values are often plotted against the values of selected predictors. For instance, fitted entry probabilities from Model 3.5 of Table B.2 are plotted against graduation year for high-scoring ($IQ = 130$) and low-scoring ($IQ = 100$) college graduates in Figure 3.3. In such figures the remaining undisplayed predictors are set to their mean values, so that the fitted curves represent the specified relationship for the "average" or "typical" member of the sample. For dummy variables that describe categorical attributes of the individual, such averages represent the proportion of the sample that has a value "1" on the dummy variable. This strategy ensures that the displayed findings represent the sample as a whole (rather than, for example, specifically males or females, in the case of gender). The strategy also reduces the number of fitted plots that need to be displayed (replacing separate plots for "males" and "females," and so forth) and it ensures that summary statistics obtained from the fitted models are commensurate with other whole-sample descriptive statistics cited throughout the text.

Table B.1   Predictors included in the statistical models of Chapter 3.

Predictor	Description
NLS Young Men, Young Women, and Youth Databases	
GRADYEAR	Calendar year in which the student graduated (1967–1984, inclusive). Originally treated as a sequence of dummy variables, but preliminary analyses demonstrated that a continuous representation was appropriate.
RACE	Race of the graduate (0 = White, 1 = Black).
GENDER	Gender of the graduate (0 = Male, 1 = Female).
AGE	Dummy variable representing age at graduation (0 = less than 24 years old, 1 = age 24 or older). Originally treated as a continuous variable, but dichotomized on the basis of preliminary analyses.
COLLEGE MAJOR	Seven dummy variables representing the student's undergraduate major (EDUCATION, HUMANITIES, MATHEMATICS, SOCIAL SCIENCES, SCIENCE, BUSINESS, OTHER).
IQ	Graduate's intelligence quotient (IQ) score.
AFQT	Graduate's score on the Armed Forces Qualifications Test (NLS Youth data set only).
North Carolina Database	
LICENSYR	Calendar year in which the graduate was licensed as a teacher in North Carolina (1974–1985, inclusive). Preliminary analyses treating LICENSYR as a sequence of dummy variables demonstrated that a linear continuous representation was appropriate.
RACE	Race of the licensee (0 = White, 1 = Black).
AGE/GENDER	Four dummy variables representing the gender and age at which the graduate became licensed as a teacher in North Carolina (YOUNG WOMEN, YOUNG MEN, MATURE WOMEN, MATURE MEN). Preliminary analyses treating AGE as a linear continuous predictor indicated that dichotomization at age 30 was appropriate.
YOUNG WOMEN	Females of age 30 or younger when licensed.
YOUNG MEN	Males of age 30 or younger when licensed.
MATURE WOMEN	Females of age 31 or older when licensed.
MATURE MEN	Males of age 31 or older when licensed.
SUBJECT SPECIALTY	Twelve dummy variables representing the licensee's subject-area specialty (SPECIAL EDUCATION, ELEMENTARY, BIOLOGY, CHEMISTRY/PHYSICS, MATHEMATICS, ENGLISH, SOCIAL STUDIES, PHYSICAL EDUCATION, BUSINESS, MUSIC, ART, FOREIGN LANGUAGES).
NTE	The licensee's score on the Weighted Common Examination of the NTE.

Table B.2   Fitted logistic regression models describing the probability of entry into
teaching within five years of graduation, nationally. (Models 3.1–3.5 are
based on the NLS Young Men, Young Women, and Youth data sets; Model
3.6 uses only the NLS Youth data set. Sampling weights have not been
incorporated into the analyses.)

Predictors Included	Model 3.1	Model 3.2	Model 3.3	Model 3.4	Model 3.5	Model 3.6
INTERCEPT	6.79**	6.21**	7.82**	9.77**	−1.94**	−0.47
GRADYEAR	−0.11**	−0.10**	−0.13**	−0.13**	−0.12**	−0.03
RACE		5.35*	6.64**	3.09	0.04	−1.34*
RACE by GRADYEAR		−0.07*	−0.08*	−0.04	−0.12⁻	−0.69*
GENDER			1.60**	1.09**	1.64**	1.28**
AGE				−0.63**	−0.63**	−0.25
COLLEGE MAJOR (Baseline−EDUCATION):						
HUMANITIES				−1.76**		
MATHEMATICS				−1.44**		
SOCIAL SCIENCES				−2.65**		
SCIENCE				−2.20**		
BUSINESS				−3.02**		
OTHER				−2.29**		
IQ					−0.03**	
IQ^2					−0.0005⁻	
IQ by GRADYEAR					−0.004*	
AFQT						−0.02*
Baseline χ^2 statistic	2,791	2,791	2,791	2,791	1,771	464
Change in χ^2 statistic	128	146	385	811	241	38
Number of graduates	2,539	2,539	2,539	2,539	1,485	682

⁻ $p < .10$.   * $p < .05$.   ** $p < .01$.

In the second section of Chapter 3, we examine entry into public school teaching within three years of being licensed as a teacher in North Carolina. In this state during the time period under study, two types of teaching license—"provisional" and "continuing"—were granted to aspiring teachers. In the main text we describe trends, by year of licensure, in the raw entry frequencies and percentages for both types of licensee. Then, for continuing licensees only, we use logit analysis to summarize the relationship between a dichotomous outcome variable ("entered teaching within three years of licensure" versus "did not enter teaching within three years of licensure") and selected characteristics of the licensees (Table B.1).

Our analytic strategies were identical to those described above for the national database, and a hierarchy of important fitted models is presented in Table B.3. Model 3.7 includes predictors describing year of licensure and personal character-

Table B.3 Fitted logistic regression models describing the probability of entry into teaching in North Carolina within three years of licensure.

Predictors Included	Model 3.7	Model 3.8	Model 3.9
INTERCEPT	1.06**	1.40**	1.43**
LICENSYR	−0.01	−0.08**	−0.08**
LICENSYR^2	−0.02**	−0.02**	−0.02**
RACE	−0.09	−0.01	−0.13
RACE by LICENSYR	−0.02	−0.02	−0.02
AGE/GENDER (Baseline−MATURE WOMEN):			
YOUNG WOMEN	−0.34**	−0.38**	−0.41**
YOUNG MEN	−0.76**	−0.32**	−0.33**
MATURE MEN	−0.97**	−0.66**	−0.65**
LICENSYR by YOUNG WOMEN	−0.09**	−0.08**	−0.09**
RACE by YOUNG WOMEN	−0.08	0.20	0.22
RACE by YOUNG MEN	0.35*	0.44*	0.45*
RACE by YOUNG WOMEN by LICENSYR	0.11**	0.09*	0.09*
SUBJECT SPECIALTY (Baseline−ELEMENTARY):			
SPECIAL EDUCATION		0.29**	0.31**
BIOLOGY		−0.36**	−0.29**
CHEMISTRY/PHYSICS		−0.64**	−0.52**
MATHEMATICS		−0.20**	−0.13⁻
ENGLISH		−0.68**	−0.59**
SOCIAL STUDIES		−1.18**	−1.12**
PHYSICAL EDUCATION		−1.09**	−1.14**
BUSINESS		−1.73**	−1.78**
MUSIC		−0.92**	−0.91**
ART		−0.95**	−0.95**
FOREIGN LANGUAGES		−0.90**	−0.82**
LICENSYR by SUBJECT SPECIALTY:			
LICENSYR by SPECIAL EDUCATION		0.05*	0.04⁻
LICENSYR by BIOLOGY		0.09**	0.09**
LICENSYR by CHEMISTRY/PHYSICS		0.14*	0.15*
LICENSYR by MATHEMATICS		0.13**	0.12**
LICENSYR by ENGLISH		0.08**	0.08**
LICENSYR by SOCIAL STUDIES		0.11**	0.10**
LICENSYR by PHYSICAL EDUCATION		0.08**	0.08**
LICENSYR by BUSINESS		0.11**	0.11**
LICENSYR by MUSIC		0.07**	0.07**
LICENSYR by ART		0.07*	0.08*
LICENSYR by FOREIGN LANGUAGES		0.15**	0.15**
RACE by SUBJECT SPECIALTY:			
RACE by SPECIAL EDUCATION		−0.34*	−0.33*
RACE by BIOLOGY		−0.42⁻	−0.48*
RACE by CHEMISTRY/PHYSICS		−1.78	−1.80

Table B.3 (continued)

Predictors Included	Model 3.7	Model 3.8	Model 3.9
RACE by MATHEMATICS		−0.17	−0.22
RACE by ENGLISH		−0.03	−0.09
RACE by SOCIAL STUDIES		0.26⁻	0.22
RACE by PHYSICAL EDUCATION		−0.16	−0.11
RACE by BUSINESS		−0.80**	−0.77**
RACE by MUSIC		−0.60**	−0.60**
RACE by ART		0.29	0.30
RACE by FOREIGN LANGUAGES		0.84⁻	0.83⁻
NTE			−0.16**
NTE²			−0.06**
Baseline χ^2 statistic	40,219	40,219	40,219
Change in χ^2 statistic	616	2,507	2,599
Number of licensees	30,571	30,571	30,571

⁻ $p < .10$.　　*$p < .05$.　　**$p < .01$.

istics of the licensees (race, gender). Model 3.8 adds the licensee's subject-area specialty, and Model 3.9 adds his or her standardized test score.

Statistical Analyses: Chapter 5

In Chapter 5 we investigate the relationship between career duration and characteristics of the teachers and the conditions under which they are employed. Our findings are based on the careers of 6,935 full-time teachers who started their careers in the Michigan public schools between 1972 and 1975, and 9,644 full-time teachers with continuing licenses and scores on the NTE who began their careers in the North Carolina public schools between 1974 and 1978. These state-based findings are buttressed by analyses of the career paths of a national sample of 625 college graduates, drawn from the NLS Young Men and Young Women databases, who became teachers between 1967 and 1987. For every teacher, we know the duration of the "first teaching spell"—the number of years taught continuously between the year they were first hired as teachers and when they quit.

Analyses of career duration are made difficult by data limitations that jeopardize the interpretation of the results.[2] The central dilemma concerns the analytic treatment of *right-censored* teachers, those still employed when data collection ends. The careers of more than half the teachers in our samples were censored. We do not know how long they remained as teachers after data collection ended; we only know that their first spells did not terminate within the period of our observation. If we were to set aside the censored teachers and focus only on teachers whose first spells terminated before data collection ended, we would misrepresent the true distribution of career duration. The very existence of censored (that is, continuing) teachers indicates, for example, that aggregate first-spell duration must be longer than that found only among teachers who have already left. Data on continuing teachers tell us much about the probability that teachers will remain longer than the duration of the data collection. Accurate analyses of first-spell duration must include censored cases, even though their first-spell durations are unknown.

Censored teachers were incorporated into our analyses by the use of *survival analysis*.[3] Under this approach we examine the *hazard function,* a mathematical transformation of first-spell duration that remains meaningful in the face of censoring. Hazard is related to the probability that a teacher will stop teaching in a specific year, given that she or he has taught up to that year.[4] Perhaps the simplest way to conceptualize hazard is visually, as a plot over time—a profile describing the probability of terminating a first spell in any particular year, given that the teacher has persisted up to that year. The hazard profile indicates how likely it is that the first spell will terminate in any given year.

By comparing the magnitude of the hazard profile from year to year we can determine if there are particular years in which a teacher is more "at risk" of terminating a first spell. If a large proportion of teachers leave the profession at the end of their first year, then the hazard will be high—reflecting the increased likelihood that the first spell will terminate after one year. If, during some other interval—perhaps the seventh or eighth years after entry—relatively few of the remaining teachers leave, then hazard will be small and we can conclude that this time period is not risky at all.

By comparing hazard profiles for teachers of different races, genders, subject-area specialties, and so forth, we can determine whether the risk of leaving teaching is more, or less, associated with teachers' background, training, and environment. In practice, such comparisons are achieved by including single or multiple predictors in statistical models for the hazard profile, in much the same way that predictors are included in the more familiar regression models. Unlike regression analysis, however, survival analysis allows us to examine the effects of predictors, such as salary, that themselves vary over time ("time-varying covariates"). And because interactions between predictors and time itself are also permitted as predictors in the models, we can investigate whether the *effects* of selected predictors are constant or vary systematically as the teaching career progresses. This latter feature allows us to examine, for example, whether salary is more strongly related to the risk of leaving teaching among beginning teachers than among experienced teachers.

Because we measured career duration discretely—the details of a teacher's career only being known to us at the end of each academic year—we have employed *discrete-time survival analysis*.[5] Thus, in our work, hazard is indeed defined as the probability that a teacher will leave the profession in a particular year, given that she or he remained on the job until that year. In the text, in order to avoid negative connotations associated with the term "hazard," we have referred to these conditional probabilities as the "risk of leaving teaching."

An additional advantage of the discrete-time approach is that the parameters of the hazard model can easily be estimated using standard logistic regression analysis routines after minor data manipulation. John Willett and Judith Singer, in a separate publication, explain this process in detail, providing examples of how such analyses are actually conducted and describing the required data manipulation.[6] Because we have used discrete-time survival analysis, our findings are summarized in this appendix as tables of fitted logistic regression models.

In Chapter 5 survival analysis is used to explore the relationship between first-spell duration and selected predictors (Table B.4). Among the predictors included in our hazard models were: (1) dummy variables to represent the duration of the first teaching spell (as required by the discrete-time approach), (2) dummy variables identifying the entering cohort in which the teacher belongs, (3) descriptors of the socioeconomic and demographic characteristics of the first school district in which each teacher was employed, (4) personal attributes of the teacher (race, gender, and age at entry into teaching), (5) the teacher's subject-area specialty and standardized test score, and (6) the teacher's salary stream.

Parallel analyses were conducted in the Michigan and North Carolina databases, and supplementary analyses were carried out in the national database. In each case a hierarchy of hazard models was built systematically in the same manner that we described for the logistic regression models of Chapter 3. A selection of fitted models is provided in Tables B.5, B.6, and B.7, presenting, respectively, our principal findings for Michigan, North Carolina, and nationally.

To construct each hierarchy, we began by examining models that included selected predictors that were known to be associated with employment duration (entry cohort, race, characteristics of the school district, age at entry into teaching, and gender). Building on these initial models, we then examined the relationship between hazard and: (1) subject-area specialty and salary (in Michigan, Models 5.4, 5.5 and 5.6), (2) subject-area specialty, salary and standardized test score (in North Carolina, Models 5.10, 5.11, 5.12 and 5.13), (3) standardized test score (nationally, Model 5.14). Wherever appropriate, we evaluated the effects of two-way and higher-order interactions among predictors.

In Michigan (Table B.5) and North Carolina (Table B.6), Models 5.2, 5.3, 5.8, and 5.9 were fitted so that we could test "fixed-effects" or "district-specific" hypotheses about the relative career durations of Black and White teachers in two different settings. In Models 5.2 and 5.8 we examine, for Michigan and North Carolina, respectively, the risk of ending a first spell among teachers of either race *in school districts that hired both Black and White teachers* in the period under study. In Models 5.3 and 5.9 we examine, again in Michigan and North Carolina, respectively, the risk of ending a first spell among teachers *in school districts that hired White teachers exclusively* (hence in these latter models the RACE predictor has been omitted). This strategy, in conjunction with the "fixed-effects"

Table B.4   Predictors included in the statistical models of Chapter 5.

Predictor	Description
Michigan and North Carolina Databases	
FIRSTSPELL	Dummy variables representing the duration of the first teaching spell (YEAR1, . . . , YEAR12). In some statistical interactions, FIRSTSPELL is treated as a linear continuous variable called LFIRSTSPELL.
COHORT	Dummy variables representing the year in which teaching began (Michigan: 1972, . . . , 1974; North Carolina: 1974, . . . , 1978). In some statistical interactions COHORT is treated as a linear continuous variable called LCOHORT.
DISTRICT	Set of dummy variables distinguishing between school districts (524 in Michigan, 121 in North Carolina).
DISTCHAR	1980 U.S. Census variables describing the aggregate demographic characteristics of each school district:
PMINOR80	Proportion of the population that is minority.
PCPOOR80	Proportion of children who are poor.
PPROF80	Proportion of workers who are professionals.
MEDINC80	Median family income in thousands of 1980 dollars.
MEDEDUC80	Median adult level of education in years.
RACE	Race of the entrant (0 = White, 1 = Black).
AGE/GENDER	Four dummy variables representing gender and age at entry into teaching (YOUNG WOMEN, YOUNG MEN, MATURE WOMEN, MATURE MEN). Preliminary analyses with AGE as a linear continuous predictor indicated that dichotomization at age 30 was appropriate.
YOUNG WOMEN	Females of age 30, or younger, on entry.
YOUNG MEN	Males of age 30, or younger, on entry.
MATURE WOMEN	Females of age 31, or older, on entry.
MATURE MEN	Males of age 31, or older, on entry.
SUBJECT SPECIALTY	Six dummy variables representing the entrant's subject-area specialty (ELEMENTARY, BIOLOGY, CHEMISTRY/PHYSICS, MATHEMATICS, ENGLISH, SOCIAL STUDIES).
SALARY	Teacher's yearly salary in thousands of 1988 dollars.
NTE	Teacher's score on the Weighted Common Examination of the NTE (North Carolina only).
NLS Young Men and Young Women Databases	
FIRSTSPELL	Sequence of dummy variables representing the duration of the first teaching spell (YEAR1, . . . , YEAR15).
GENDER	Gender of the entrant (0 = Male, 1 = Female).
RACE	Race of the entrant (0 = White, 1 = Black).
IQ	Entrant's Intelligence Quotient

approach described below, allows us to ask whether the career durations of Black and White teachers are intrinsically different or whether any extant differences are attributable to a selection process that filters Black teachers disproportionately into certain types of school districts—in this case, the large urban districts—in which the career durations of *all* teachers are shorter, regardless of race.

In fixed-effects analyses, dummy variables that distinguish each school district from every other district are included as control predictors in the model to allow the relationship between hazard and other key predictors to be examined as though all teachers were employed in the same school district.[7] These fixed-effects discrete-time hazard models were fitted by a linear probability, rather than a logistic, approach because the addition of several hundred "school district" dummies created models that were too cumbersome for iterative nonlinear estimation.[8] In all subsequent models, control for school district was achieved by including six predictors describing the socioeconomic and demographic characteristics of each district. The discrete-time logistic regression approach was then again used to fit these models (Models 5.4–5.6, 5.10–5.13).

To illustrate our findings in the text, we frequently display fitted hazard profiles (with the vertical axis labeled "risk of leaving," as explained above). Such plots are the conceptual equivalent of the fitted relationships that can be displayed following multiple regression analysis, and they permit inspection of the predicted relationship between the risk of leaving teaching and first-spell duration for different types of teachers. In Figure 5.2, for instance, we plot the risk of terminating a first teaching job against first-spell duration for secondary school teachers in low, average, and high salary streams. For reasons outlined earlier, these fitted hazard profiles were constructed by setting the undisplayed predictors to their mean values so that the relationship is displayed for the "average" or "typical" member of the sample.

In the main text, we often use a *median first-spell duration* or a *five-year survival probability* as a single-number summary of the hazard profile. The median first-spell duration estimates the number of years that must pass before half of any given group of teachers leave teaching. Median first-spell duration is a useful summary of the hazard profile because it permits the research questions, which were originally framed in terms of duration, to be answered in the same metric. The five-year survival probability is an alternative summary statistic that estimates the probability that a randomly selected teacher will remain in teaching until the end of the fifth year of the first spell.

When the first-spell durations of the majority of the teachers in a sample are longer than the length of data collection, we may not be able to estimate a specific value for median first-spell duration other than by stating it to be longer than the period of data collection. In these cases, it is more informative to make use of the five-year survival probability. These two summary statistics are intimately linked together; teachers who are at the greatest risk of terminating a first spell must necessarily have shorter careers and lower five-year survival probabilities. In the text we make use of whichever of these three summaries—the fitted hazard

Table B.5 Fitted hazard models describing the risk of ending a first teaching spell in Michigan.

Predictors Included	Model 5.1	Model 5.2	Model 5.3	Model 5.4	Model 5.5	Model 5.6
INTERCEPT	−1.27**	.703**	1.000**	−1.64*	−1.27⁻	−1.36⁻
FIRSTSPELL (Baseline−YEAR1):						
YEAR2	−0.59**	−.081**	−.049**	−0.55**	−0.56**	−0.54**
YEAR3	−0.63**	−.073**	−.043**	−0.56**	−0.58**	−0.56**
YEAR4	−0.67**	−.072**	−.040**	−0.58**	−0.59**	−0.61**
YEAR5	−0.71**	−.077**	−.035**	−0.59**	−0.62**	−0.68**
YEAR6	−0.84**	−.053**	−.050**	−0.70**	−0.73**	−0.88**
YEAR7	−0.93**	−.048**	−.055**	−0.77**	−0.81**	−1.04**
YEAR8	−1.19**	−.052**	−.074**	−1.02**	−1.05**	−1.34**
YEAR9	−1.48**	−.079**	−.085**	−1.31**	−1.35**	−1.69**
YEAR10	−1.69**	−.101**	−.088**	−1.52**	−1.56**	−1.99**
YEAR11	−2.07**	−.114**	−.105**	−1.90**	−1.95**	−2.49**
YEAR12	−2.13**	−.140**	−.101**	−2.00**	−2.06**	−2.71**
COHORT (Baseline−1972):						
1973	−0.07⁻	.010	−.005	−0.05	−0.06	−0.20**
1974	−0.16**	−.005	−.010⁻	−0.15**	−0.15**	−0.40**
1975	0.01	.024*	.011⁻	0.01	0.02	−0.28**
DISTRICT		included	included			
RACE		.049*		0.34*	0.33⁻	0.41*
RACE by LFIRSTSPELL		−.028**		−0.28**	−0.28**	−0.31**
RACE by LFIRSTSPELL^2		.002*		0.02**	0.02**	0.03**

DISTCHAR:						
PMINOR80				1.19**	1.21**	1.26**
PCPOOR80				0.36	0.33	0.34
PPROF80				−0.85*	−0.87*	−0.96*
MEDINC80				0.00	0.00	0.00
MEDEDUC80				−0.03	−0.03	−0.04
AGE/GENDER (Baseline–MATURE WOMEN):						
YOUNG WOMEN				0.71**	0.71**	0.73**
YOUNG MEN				0.14^{-}	0.13^{-}	0.16*
MATURE MEN				0.05	0.04	0.08
SUBJECT SPECIALTY:						
ELEMENTARY					−0.38**	
BIOLOGY				0.25**		0.32**
CHEMISTRY/PHYSICS				0.91**		0.96**
MATHEMATICS				0.56**		0.64**
ENGLISH				0.42**		0.48**
SOCIAL STUDIES				0.35**		0.41**
LFIRSTSPELL by MATHEMATICS				−0.06*		−0.06*
SALARY						−0.77**
SALARY^2						0.07**
SALARY by LFIRSTSPELL						0.08**
SALARY^2 by LFIRSTSPELL						−0.01**
SALARY by COHORT						0.11**
SALARY by ELEMENTARY						0.07*
Baseline χ^2 statistic	29,199	—	—	29,199	29,199	29,199
Change in χ^2 statistic	964	—	—	1,536	1,513	1,647
Number of (person-year) observations	40,179	9,727	30,447	40,179	40,179	40,179

$^{-}$ $p < .10$.   * $p < .05$.   ** $p < .01$.

Table B.6 Fitted hazard models describing the risk of ending a first teaching spell in North Carolina.

Predictors Included	Model 5.7	Model 5.8	Model 5.9	Model 5.10	Model 5.11	Model 5.12	Model 5.13
INTERCEPT	−1.94**	.101**	.093**	−2.11**	−1.54*	−2.22**	−2.64**
FIRSTSPELL (Baseline—YEAR1):							
YEAR2	−0.35**	−.029**	−.051**	−0.35**	−0.42**	−0.35**	−0.29**
YEAR3	−0.40**	−.032**	−.051**	−0.40**	−0.53**	−0.39**	−0.26**
YEAR4	−0.49**	−.039**	−.033*	−0.50**	−0.70**	−0.49**	−0.29**
YEAR5	−0.54**	−.039**	−.076**	−0.56**	−0.83**	−0.55**	−0.31**
YEAR6	−0.72**	−.050**	−.068**	−0.76**	−1.09**	−0.74**	−0.45**
YEAR7	−0.74**	−.049**	−.083**	−0.79**	−1.19**	−0.77**	−0.44**
YEAR8	−1.12**	−.067**	−.084**	−1.20**	−1.66**	−1.18**	−0.83**
YEAR9	−1.16**	−.067**	−.083**	−1.27**	−1.79**	−1.24**	−0.89**
YEAR10	−1.09**	−.063**	−.090**	−1.21**	−1.80**	−1.19**	−0.89**
YEAR11	−1.25**	−.074**	−.080*	−1.37**	−2.02**	−1.35**	−1.15**
COHORT (Baseline—1974):							
1975	−0.28**	−.019**	−.015	−0.29**	−0.30**	−0.29**	−0.33**
1976	−0.16**	−.012**	−.005	−0.16**	−0.16**	−0.15**	−0.19**
1977	−0.02	−.001	.003	−0.02	−0.01	−0.01	−0.06
1978	−0.08⁻	−.005	−.007	−0.08	−0.08	−0.05	−0.15*
DISTRICT		included	included				
RACE		−.038**		−0.34**	−0.34**	−0.09	−0.09

	(1)	(2)	(3)	(4)	(5)
RACE by LFIRSTSPELL	−.000	−0.09**	−0.09**	−0.09**	−0.09**
DISTCHAR:					
PMINOR80		1.00**	0.99**	0.95**	0.93**
PCPOOR80		−1.63**	−1.68**	−1.35*	−1.16⁻
PPROF80		3.30**	3.29**	2.88**	2.86**
MEDINC80		−0.00	−0.00	−0.00	0.00
MEDEDUC80		−0.07	−0.07	−0.06	−0.06
AGE/GENDER (Baseline—MATURE WOMEN):					
YOUNG WOMEN		0.22*	0.19	0.24*	0.24*
YOUNG MEN		0.39**	0.35*	0.37**	0.37**
MATURE MEN		0.21	0.12	0.15	0.17
LFIRSTSPELL by YOUNG WOMEN		0.06**	0.06**	0.06**	0.06**
SUBJECT SPECIALTY:			−0.63**		
ELEMENTARY					
BIOLOGY		1.38**		1.27**	1.31**
CHEMISTRY/PHYSICS		0.47		0.28	0.28
MATHEMATICS		0.24		0.04	0.06
ENGLISH		0.89**		0.73**	0.75**
SOCIAL STUDIES		0.07		−0.02	0.00
LFIRSTSPELL by BIOLOGY		−0.08*		−0.08*	−0.08**
LFIRSTSPELL by CHEMISTRY/PHYSICS		−0.02		−0.02	−0.02
LFIRSTSPELL by MATHEMATICS		−0.04		−0.04	−0.04
LFIRSTSPELL by ENGLISH		−0.09**		−0.09**	−0.09**

Table B.6 (continued)

Predictors Included	Model 5.7	Model 5.8	Model 5.9	Model 5.10	Model 5.11	Model 5.12	Model 5.13
LFIRSTSPELL by SOCIAL STUDIES				−0.04		−0.04	−0.04⁻
YOUNG WOMEN by BIOLOGY				−0.62⁻		−0.62⁻	−0.65⁻
YOUNG WOMEN by CHEMISTRY/PHYSICS				0.11		0.15	0.14
YOUNG WOMEN by MATHEMATICS				0.00		0.09	0.09
YOUNG WOMEN by ENGLISH				−0.11		−0.09	−0.10
YOUNG WOMEN by SOCIAL STUDIES				0.41		0.40	0.39
YOUNG MEN by BIOLOGY				−0.82*		−0.77*	−0.80*
YOUNG MEN by CHEMISTRY/PHYSICS				0.71		0.70	0.71
YOUNG MEN by MATHEMATICS				0.33		0.46	0.46
YOUNG MEN by ENGLISH				−0.11		−0.12	−0.13
YOUNG MEN by SOCIAL STUDIES				0.29		0.30	0.30
ELEMENTARY by LFIRSTSPELL					0.07**		
ELEMENTARY by YOUNG WOMEN					0.04		
ELEMENTARY by YOUNG MEN					0.04		
NTE						0.28**	0.28**
NTE²						0.05**	0.06**
SALARY							−0.42**
SALARY by LFIRSTSPELL							0.07**
Baseline χ² statistic	32,320	—	—	32,320	32,320	32,320	32,320
Change in χ² statistic	512	—	—	1,161	1,111	1,323	1,336
Number of (person-year) observations	61,874	58,388	3,452	61,874	61,874	61,874	61,874

⁻ $p < .10$.   * $p < .05$.   ** $p < .01$.

Table B.7 Fitted hazard models describing the risk of ending a first teaching spell nationally. (Based on the NLS Young Men and Young Women data sets. No sampling weights included.)

Predictors Included	Model 5.14
INTERCEPT	−2.38**
FIRSTSPELL (Baseline−YEAR1):	
YEAR2	−0.16
YEAR3	−0.16
YEAR4	−0.78**
YEAR5	−0.23
YEAR6	−0.51*
YEAR7	−0.45⁻
YEAR8	−0.73*
YEAR9	−0.87*
YEAR10	−0.67⁻
YEAR11	−1.77**
YEAR12	−0.78⁻
YEAR13	−0.61
YEAR14	−0.23
YEAR15	−0.31
RACE	−0.03
GENDER	−0.39**
IQ	0.01*
Baseline χ^2 statistic	2,004
Change in χ^2 statistic	51
Number of (person-year) observations	2,345

⁻ $p < .10.$ * $p < .05.$ ** $p < .01.$

profile, the median first-spell duration, or the five-year survival probability—is the most convenient for describing our findings.

Statistical Analyses: Chapter 6

In Chapter 6 we examine the career behavior of Michigan and North Carolina teachers who ended a first teaching spell prior to the final two years of observation, and who were therefore eligible to return to teaching during the period covered by our study. Because each teacher was tracked for a finite number of years, it was inappropriate to classify all teachers who had not returned by the end of data collection as "nonreturners." There always remained the possibility that these teachers would return to teaching after our data collection ended. To resolve this problem, teachers who had not returned by the end of data collection were treated as right-censored. We reframed our research question from "Who returns?" to "How long do they stay out?" so that survival analysis could be used to examine "time out of teaching" in the same way that first-spell duration was investigated in Chapter 5. In the text, to avoid negative connotations associated with the terms "risk" and "hazard," we use the phrase "rate of reentry" to refer to the probability that a former teacher will return to teaching in any particular year, given that she had not yet returned before that year.

Our findings are based on the careers of the 4,676 full-time teachers in the Michigan public schools and the 4,283 full-time teachers (with continuing licenses and scores on the NTE) in the North Carolina public schools who had earlier terminated a first spell. For each of these teachers, we know the "time out of teaching" after the first spell ended. The state databases contain no information on the occupational experiences of former teachers. This information is available, however, for 456 former teachers in the NLS Young Men, Young Women, and Youth data sets. In Chapter 6, we use these data to explore whether a return to teaching depends upon the type of employment taken after the first spell was terminated.

In Chapter 6, then, discrete-time survival analysis is used to explore the relationship between time out of teaching and selected predictors (Table B.8). Among the predictors included in our models were: (1) dummy variables to represent the duration of the time out of teaching (as required by the discrete-time approach), (2) dummy variables identifying the exit cohort to which the teacher belonged, (3) personal attributes of the teacher (race, gender, and age at termination of first spell), (5) the teacher's subject-area specialty and standardized test score, and (6) the teacher's occupation while out of teaching.

As before, parallel analyses were conducted in the Michigan and North Carolina databases with supplementary analyses being carried out in the national database. For each database, a hierarchy of hazard models was built in the same manner as described for Chapter 5. A selection of important fitted models is provided in Tables B.9, B.10, and B.11 representing our principal findings for Michigan, North Carolina, and nationally, respectively. In each case we began by examining models that included control predictors and demographic characteristics (exit cohort, race, age at termination of first spell, and gender). Building on these initial models, we then examined the relationship between hazard and: (1) subject-area specialty (in Michigan, Models 6.2 and 6.3), (2) subject-area specialty and standardized test score (in North Carolina, Models 6.5, 6.6, and 6.7), (3) type of job acquired while out of teaching (nationally, Model 6.8). Wherever appropriate, we evaluated the effects of two-way and higher-order interactions among predictors.

Table B.8   Predictors included in the statistical models of Chapter 6.

Predictor	Description
Michigan and North Carolina Databases	
TIMEOUT	Sequence of dummy variables representing the number of years spent out of teaching (Michigan: YEAR1, . . . , YEAR11; North Carolina: YEAR1, . . . , YEAR10).
EXIT COHORT	Sequence of dummy variables representing the calendar year in which the first spell was terminated (Michigan: 1973, . . . , 1983; North Carolina: 1975, . . . , 1984).
RACE	Race of the teacher (0 = White, 1 = Black).
AGE/GENDER	Four dummy variables representing the gender and age at which the individual terminated a first spell in teaching (YOUNG WOMEN, YOUNG MEN, MATURE WOMEN, MATURE MEN). Preliminary analyses with AGE as a linear continuous predictor indicated that dichotomization at age 30 was appropriate.
YOUNG WOMEN	Females of age 30 or younger at end of first spell.
YOUNG MEN	Males of age 30 or younger at end of first spell.
MATURE WOMEN	Females of age 31 or older at end of first spell.
MATURE MEN	Males of 31 or older at end of first spell.
SUBJECT SPECIALTY	Six dummy variables representing the teacher's subject-area specialty (ELEMENTARY, BIOLOGY, CHEMISTRY/PHYSICS, MATHEMATICS, ENGLISH, SOCIAL STUDIES).
NTE	The teacher's score on the Weighted Common Examination of the NTE (North Carolina only).
NLS Young Men, Young Women, and Youth Databases	
TIMEOUT	Sequence of dummy variables representing the number of years spent out of teaching (YEAR1, . . . , YEAR9).
EXITYEAR	Year in which the first spell was terminated. Preliminary analyses indicated that exit year could be treated as linear continuous variable.
RACE	Race of the teacher (0 = White, 1 = Black).
GENDER	Gender of the teacher (0 = Male, 1 = Female).
PROFESSIONAL	The type of job entered after termination of a first spell in teaching (0 = Nonprofessional, 1 = Professional).

Table B.11   Fitted hazard models describing the rate of reentry into teaching nationally. (Based on the NLS Young Men, Young Women, and Youth data sets. No sampling weights included.)

Predictors Included	Model 6.8
INTERCEPT	4.81
TIMEOUT (Baseline−YEAR1):	
YEAR2	−0.15
YEAR3	−0.96*
YEAR4	−2.07**
YEAR5	−1.59**
YEAR6	−1.70**
YEAR7	−1.97**
YEAR8	−8.76
YEAR9	−0.79
EXITYEAR	−0.09*
RACE	0.49⁻
GENDER	−11.40*
PROFESSIONAL	0.59*
GENDER by EXITYEAR	0.15**
Baseline χ^2 statistic	633
Change in χ^2 statistic	73
Number of (person-year) observations	1,223

$^-p < .10.$ $*p < .05.$ $**p < .01.$

Notes

1. The Teaching Profession at a Turning Point

1. See Debra E. Gerald, Paul J. Horn, and William J. Hussar, *Projections of Education Statistics to 2000* (Washington, D.C.: National Center for Education Statistics, U.S. Department of Education, 1989), p. 78. We cite the intermediate projection of 2.3 million newly hired teachers. There are also high and low projections.

2. As of 1988 there were 2.1 million accountants, lawyers, judges, and physicians working in the United States. See *The Occupational Outlook Handbook*, Bulletin 2350 (Washington, D.C.: U.S. Department of Labor, April 1990).

3. The U.S. Department of Education projected that 1.7 million new elementary and secondary school teachers would be hired between 1980 and 1990. See Martin M. Frankel and Debra E. Gerald, *Projections of Education Statistics to 1990–91* (Washington, D.C.: National Center for Education Statistics, U.S. Department of Education, 1982), pp. 82 and 84.

4. Gerald, Horn, and Hussar, *Projections of Education Statistics to 2000*, p. 11.

5. *A Nation Prepared: Teachers for the 21st Century*, report of the Task Force on Teaching as a Profession (New York: Carnegie Forum on Education and the Economy, 1986), pp. 2 and 7.

6. *N.E.A. Bulletin*, 8, no. 3 (November 1919), 14.

7. As Michael Sedlak and Stephen Schlossman point out in *Who Will Teach? Historical Perspectives on the Changing Appeal of Teaching as a Profession* (Santa Monica, Calif.: RAND Corporation, 1986), the educational qualifications of the teaching force have increased markedly during this century. This occurred during a period when the average educational attainments of the population were also rising rapidly. Consequently, Sedlak and Schlossman's evidence is consistent with our assertion that the status of the teaching profession relative to that of other professions has not improved.

8. "National Goals for Education," The White House, Washington, D.C., February 26, 1990.

9. All dollar figures are expressed in 1988 constant dollars. The estimates of average starting salary were provided by F. Howard Nelson, Associate Director of Re-

search, American Federation of Teachers, Washington, D.C. The salary estimates come from surveys conducted by Educational Research Service.

10. See, for example, National Education Association, (NEA), *Status of the American Public School Teacher: 1985–86* (Washington, D.C.: NEA, 1987); Metropolitan Life Insurance Company, *The Metropolitan Life Survey of Former Teachers in America* (New York: Metropolitan Life Insurance Company, 1986); and Metropolitan Life Insurance Company, *Metropolitan Life Survey of the American Teacher* (New York: Metropolitan Life Insurance Company, 1988).

11. Metropolitan Life Insurance Company, *Metropolitan Life Survey.*

12. Stephen M. Barro, *International Comparisons of Teachers' Salaries: An Exploratory Study,* report prepared for the U.S. Department of Education (Washington, D.C.: U.S. Department of Education, 1987). An exception is Hawaii, whose education system is run by the state.

13. These calculations are based on salary data provided by the College Placement Council and the American Federation of Teachers. It is important to point out that trends over the 1970s in the earnings of teachers relative to the earnings of college graduates in business and industry vary by college major. For example, the constant dollar starting salaries of humanities majors entering business and industry fell by approximately the same percentage that real starting salaries in teaching fell. As explained in the text, the decline in the number of job openings in teaching during the 1970s made this occupational choice increasingly unattractive to well-educated college graduates in any field.

14. See the plaintiffs' briefs in the many court cases in which residents of property-poor school districts argue that inadequate financing of public schools denies their children access to high-quality education.

15. Eric A. Hanushek, "Throwing Money at Schools," *Journal of Policy Analysis and Management,* 1, no. 1 (1981), 19–41. Quotation is from page 19.

16. See U.S. National Commission for Excellence in Education, *A Nation At Risk* (Washington, D.C.: U.S. Government Printing Office, 1983); American Association for the Advancement of Science (AAAS), *Project 2061: Science for All Americans* (Washington, D.C.: AAAS, 1989); and National Center for Education Statistics, *The Condition of Education, 1989,* vol. 1, (Washington, D.C.: U.S. Department of Education, 1989).

17. See, for example, U.S. General Accounting Office, *New Directions for Federal Programs to Aid Mathematics and Science Teaching* (Washington, D.C.: U.S. Government Printing Office, 1984); Russell Rumberger, "The Shortage of Mathematics and Science Teachers: A Review of the Evidence," *Educational Evaluation and Policy Analysis,* 7, no. 4 (1985), 355–369; Henry M. Levin, "Solving the Shortage of Mathematics and Science Teachers," *Educational Evaluation and Policy Analysis,* 7, no. 4 (1985), 371–382; and Office of Technology Assessment, *Educating Scientists and Engineers: Grade School to Grad School,* OTA-SET-377 (Washington, D.C.: U.S. Government Printing Office, 1988).

18. Joseph A. Kershaw and Roland N. McKean, *Teacher Shortages and Salary Schedules* (New York: McGraw-Hill, 1962).

19. As indicated in note 9, the information on starting salaries for teachers comes from surveys administered by Educational Research Service (ERS), and was pro-

vided by the American Federation of Teachers, Washington, D.C. The information on starting salaries in other occupations was taken from the 1968–1988 issues of the *CPC Salary Survey*, published by the College Placement Council, Bethlehem, Pennsylvania.

20. U.S. National Commission on Excellence in Education, *A Nation at Risk*, p. 22.

21. Committee for Economic Development, *Investing in Our Children: Business and the Public Schools* (Washington, D.C.: Committee for Economic Development, 1985).

22. See, for example, Dan C. Lortie, *Schoolteacher: A Sociological Study* (Chicago, Ill.: University of Chicago Press, 1975).

23. Ernest L. Boyer, *High School: A Report on Secondary Education in America* (New York: Harper and Row, 1983).

24. These figures are based on Table 2 of Kevin Murphy and Finis Welch, "Wage Differentials in the 1980s: The Role of International Trade," UNICON working paper, May 1989, p. 17.

25. We use scores on two types of standardized tests—intelligence tests, such as the Wechsler Intelligence Scales for Children and the Stanford Binet, and the general and professional knowledge subtest of the NTE. Both types of scores are positively correlated with scores on other standardized tests such as the Scholastic Achievement Test (SAT) and the Graduate Record Examination (GRE). See, for example, Jerry B. Ayers and Glenda S. Qualls, "Concurrent and Predictive Validity of the National Teacher Examinations," *Journal of Educational Research*, 73 (November/December 1979), 86–92; Linda K. Pratt, "Study of Predictors of National Teacher Examination Scores at a Predominantly Black Institution," paper presented at the Annual Forum of the Association for Institutional Research, San Diego, May 1979 (ERIC ED 174-117); Norman Wexler, *Concurrent Validity of the National Teacher Exams* (Washington, D.C.: National Institute of Education, 1975).

26. See, for example, James S. Coleman, Ernest Q. Campbell, Carol J. Hobson, James McPartland, Alexander Mood, Frederic Weinfeld, and Robert L. York, *Equality of Educational Opportunity* (Washington, D.C.: Office of Education, National Center for Educational Statistics, GPO, 1976); Eric A. Hanushek, *Education and Race* (Lexington, Mass.: D. C. Heath, 1972); Ronald Ferguson, "Teacher Salaries, Teacher Quality, and Student Performance: Texas Schools in the Mid-1980s," working paper, Malcolm Weiner Center for Social Policy, John F. Kennedy School of Government, Harvard University, 1990; and Robert P. Strauss and Elizabeth A. Sawyer, "Some New Evidence on Teacher and Student Competencies," *Economics of Education Review*, 5, no. 1 (1986), 41–48.

27. Walt Haney, George Madaus, and Amelia Kreitzer, "Charms Talismanic: Testing Teachers for the Improvement of American Education," in *Review of Research on Education*, ed. Ernst Rothkopf (Washington, D.C.: American Educational Research Association, 1987). See also Anita A. Summers and Barbara L. Wolfe, "Do Schools Make a Difference?" *American Economic Review*, 67, no. 4 (September 1977), 639–652. In this paper, these authors find that teachers' NTE scores are not positively correlated with sixth grade students' test score gains. In a later paper, these authors find that social studies teachers' scores on the social studies subtest of the NTE are positively related to their students' test score gains. However, the scores of mathematics and English teachers on the subject-specific por-

tion of the NTE are not related to their students' achievement gains. See Anita A. Summers and Barbara L. Wolfe, "Improving the Use of Empirical Research as a Policy Tool: Replication of Educational Production Functions," in *Advances in Applied Micro-Economics,* vol. 3, ed. V. Kerry Smith and Ann Dryden Witte (Greenwich, Conn.: JAI Press, 1984).

28. National Center for Education Statistics, *Digest of Education Statistics 1989* (Washington, D.C.: U.S. Department of Education, 1989).

29. See, for example, Joan C. Baratz-Snowden, "Black Participation in the Teacher Pool," paper prepared for the Carnegie Forum on Education and the Economy, January 1986; and Linda Darling-Hammond, Karen Johnson Pittman, and Cecilia Ottinger, "Career Choices for Minorities: Who Will Teach?" paper prepared for the National Education Association and the Council of Chief State School Officers Task Force on Minorities in Teaching, October 1987.

30. American Council on Education, *Eighth Annual Status Report on Minorities in Higher Education* (Washington, D.C.: American Council on Education, 1990).

31. For a detailed study of teachers' working conditions, see Susan Moore Johnson, *Teachers at Work* (New York: Basic Books, 1990).

2. Who Prepares to Teach?

1. National Board for Professional Teaching Standards, *Toward High and Rigorous Standards for the Teaching Profession* (Detroit, Mich.: National Board for Professional Teaching Standards, 1989), p. 1.

2. G. Pritchie Smith, *The Effects of Competency Testing on the Supply of Minority Teachers,* report prepared for the National Education Association and the Council of Chief State School Officers, Jacksonville, Fla., December 1987. The timing of the administration of tests varies from state to state. In some states, candidates take tests after completing a training program, as part of the application for state certification. In other states, college students must submit test scores to gain entrance to a teacher training program.

3. The percentages were calculated from a table on page 106 of Smith, *Effects of Competency Testing.*

4. North Carolina also granted licenses to an additional 34,200 people, a majority of whom had taught previously in another state. The remainder were in the following categories: administration, vocational education, and people of Hispanic, Asian, Native American, or unknown descent. We exclude these 34,200 people from our analyses in part because we wanted to focus on new entrants in academic fields and in part because some of the groups contained too few people to provide stable estimates.

5. Higher Education General Information Surveys (HEGIS), administered by the National Center for Education Statistics, Washington, D.C.

6. Ibid.

7. See Appendix A for a description of the data from the National Longitudinal Surveys.

8. Percentages based on salary data provided by the North Carolina Association of Educators and the College Placement Council, Bethlehem, Pennsylvania. In North

Carolina, the state provides the funding for a base salary scale for all teachers in the state. Approximately half the districts in the state supplement the state-specified minimum salaries.

9. See Richard J. Murnane, Judith D. Singer, and John B. Willett, "Changes in Teacher Salaries during the 1970s: The Role of School District Demographics," *Economics of Education Review*, 6, no. 4 (1987), 379–388.

10. See Table 41 in Smith, *Effects of Competency Testing*, p. 105. This table states that 15.4 percent of the teachers newly licensed in North Carolina in 1973 and 1974 were Black. The analogous percentages for 1976 and 1977 were 16.6 and 17.5. Although the pattern of the numbers in Smith's table is consistent with the pattern illustrated in Figure 2.3b, the numbers in Smith's table are lower than the numbers on which our figure is based. The likely explanation is that we exclude licensees in certain fields, such as vocational education, in which the representation of Black graduates may be especially low.

11. Smith, *Effects of Competency Testing*, pp. 134–135.

12. Throughout the rest of this chapter, we have kept separate our findings for both Black and White licensees. We have done this so that crucial similarities and differences between the two groups can be examined without distortion of the minority picture by the White majority. This separate treatment allows us to make inferences, among other things, about the extent to which changes in the number of Black licensees contributed to the well-documented national decline in the percentage of the nation's school teachers who were Black.

13. In interpreting Figure 2.4b, note that the percentage of male licensees who were under 24 years of age fell from 56 percent in 1975 to 44 percent in 1981, and then rose to 47 percent in 1982.

14. The data on the age distribution of new licensees in Connecticut was provided by Peter Prowda and Barbara Beaudin of the Connecticut State Department of Education.

15. U.S. Bureau of the Census, *Statistical Abstract of the United States: 1988* (Washington, D.C.: U.S. Department of Commerce, 1988).

16. Chemistry and physics were treated as a single subject because the number of licenses granted in each field was very small.

17. All numbers and percentages cited in this section are based on the population of college graduates who had no teaching experience in another state before obtaining licenses in North Carolina.

18. Judith D. Singer and John A. Butler, "The Education for All Handicapped Children Act: Schools as Agents of Social Reform," *Harvard Educational Review*, 57, no. 2 (May 1987), 125–152.

3. Who Becomes a Teacher?

1. James Bryant Conant, *The Education of American Teachers* (New York: McGraw-Hill, 1963), p. 229.

2. See G. Pritchie Smith, *Effects of Competency Testing on the Supply of Minority Teachers*, report prepared for the National Educational Association and the Council of Chief State School Officers (Jacksonville, Fla., December 1987), for a detailed discus-

sion of the influence of test score requirements on the number of Black college graduates obtaining teacher licenses.

3. Raw percentages based on college graduates in the NLS Young Men, Young Women, and Youth surveys, sampling weights included. We did not include nursing in the list of professional organizations because traditionally its pay and working conditions were not better than those in teaching.

4. See Frank Levy and Richard C. Michel, "Education and Income: Recent U.S. Trends," paper prepared for the Joint Economic Committee of the U.S. Congress, December 1988, pp. 13–14. The Current Population Survey is a monthly survey of approximately 60,000 households that is administered by the U.S. Census Bureau. Information from the CPS is used to provide monthly statistics on the unemployment rate and on other dimensions of labor market performance.

5. There is some evidence that male teachers earn more than female teachers with equivalent experience, despite the presence of uniform salary scales. See Valerie E. Lee and Julia B. Smith, "Gender Equity in Teachers' Salaries: A Multilevel Approach," *Educational Evaluation and Policy Analysis*, 12 (Spring 1990), 57–81. However, the reported gender-related salary differentials are much smaller than gender-related salary differentials in other sectors of the economy.

6. Table B.2, Model 3.3.

7. Table B.2, Model 3.4.

8. U.S. National Commission on Excellence in Education, *A Nation at Risk* (Washington, D.C.: U.S. Government Printing Office, 1983), p. 22.

9. Unlike the NLS Young Women and Young Men surveys, our NLS Youth data do not include IQ scores. Consequently we could not explore the relationship between the probability of entry into teaching and IQ score for individuals who graduated from college in the early 1980s.

10. The statistics reported in this paragraph are based on data from the National Longitudinal Survey of Youth. See Appendix A for more information.

11. Table B.2, Model 3.6.

12. Peter Dolton, "The Economics of UK Teacher Supply: The Graduate's Decision," *Economic Journal*, 100, no. 4 (1990), 91–104.

13. Charles F. Manski, "Academic Ability, Earnings, and the Decision to Become a Teacher: Evidence from the National Longitudinal Study of the High School Class of 1972," in *Public Sector Payrolls*, ed. David A. Wise (Chicago, Ill.: University of Chicago Press, 1987).

14. Because our data collection ended in 1985, we use three years after licensure as the cutoff point for entry into teaching. This constraint gave all those licensed between 1975 and 1982 an identical opportunity to enter teaching.

15. Raw frequency based on all college graduates who were granted a North Carolina teaching license between 1975 and 1982.

16. Wisconsin Department of Public Instruction, *Supply and Demand of Teachers in Wisconsin* (Madison, Wis.: University of Wisconsin System, 1986), as cited in Martin Haberman, "More Minority Teachers," *Phi Delta Kappan*, 70, no. 10 (June 1989), 771–776.

17. A higher percentage of Black college graduates licensed in each year from 1983 to 1985 also entered teaching in North Carolina before the end of the 1985–86 school year than was the case for White college graduates licensed in these years.

18. The battery of NTE tests taken by applicants for a North Carolina teaching license included a four-part series of common examinations: a test of professional knowledge and three tests in general education (written English expression; social studies and the fine arts; and science and mathematics). These tests were intended to cover material that was typically required for all students in teacher education. Each of the common examinations was weighted in accordance with professional judgment regarding its relative importance in preservice teacher education programs. The sum of these weighted scores was the Weighted Common Examination Total (WCET) score. It is this WCET score that we refer to in the text as a teacher's NTE score. Applicants for a teaching license in North Carolina also typically took the relevant NTE specialty-area test. We did not use these test scores in our analysis since the scores are not comparable across specialty-area tests.

19. In the years after the NTE requirement was reinstated, applicants could waive this requirement by submitting scores of 380 Verbal Ability, 410 Quantitative Ability, and 380 Analytical Ability on the Graduate Record Examination. A small number of new licensees exercised this option. (Division of Certification, North Carolina Department of Public Instruction, National Teacher Examination Regulations, Raleigh, N.C., 1985.)

20. The entry probability estimated from Model 3.9 in Table B.3 was .691 for a licensee with an NTE score of 479 (10th percentile), .672 for a licensee with an NTE score of 584 (50th percentile), and .620 for a licensee with an NTE score of 692 (90th percentile).

21. Although the relationship between NTE score and the probability of entry was the same for Black and White continuing licensees, the NTE scores of Black licensees were approximately 100 points lower, on average, than the scores for White licensees. Very few Black licensees had NTE scores at the top of the range, where score differentials had the biggest impact on the probability of entry into teaching, and therefore the NTE score of Black licensees had a negligible effect on the probability of entry. For Black graduates, the big impact of the NTE score on their probability of entry concerned whether their scores were high enough to obtain a continuing license. Low NTE scores caused many Black graduates to be granted only provisional licenses, and graduates with these licenses were much less likely to become teachers than those with continuing licenses, all else being equal.

Richard J. Murnane and Michael Schwinden, "Race, Gender, and Opportunity: Supply and Demand for New Teachers in North Carolina, 1975–1985," *Educational Evaluation and Policy Analysis*, 11, no. 2 (Summer 1989), 93–108, report that the NTE score was positively related to the probability of entry into teaching for Black licensees. Although this finding may appear to conflict with the pattern reported in this section, there is in fact no conflict. The explanation concerns the sample definition. The Murnane and Schwinden analysis treats all Black licensees as a single group, and does not distinguish between those with continuing licenses and those with provisional licenses. Black licensees with relatively high NTE scores had a higher probability of entry into teaching than did Black licensees with lower scores because the high-scoring graduates held continuing licenses, while the low-scoring graduates held provisional licenses.

4. Finding Skilled Teachers

1. Debra E. Gould, Paul J. Horn, and William J. Hussar, *Projections of Education Statistics to 2000* (Washington, D.C.: National Center for Education Statistics, U.S. Department of Education, 1989).

2. See, for example, Edward S. Cavin, Richard J. Murnane, and Randall S. Brown, "School District Responses to Enrollment Changes: The Direction of Change Matters!" *Journal of Education Finance*, 10, no. 4 (Spring 1985), 426–440.

3. Eric A. Hanushek, "The Economics of Schooling: Production and Efficiency in the Public Schools," *Journal of Economic Literature*, 24, no. 3 (September 1986), 1141–1177.

4. See, for example, Arthur E. Wise, Linda Darling-Hammond, and Barnett Berry, *Effective Teacher Selection: From Recruitment to Retention* (Santa Monica, Calif.: RAND Corporation, 1987); and Joseph Shivers, "Hiring Shortage-area and Non-shortage-area Teachers at the Secondary School Level," Ed. D. dissertation, Harvard University Graduate School of Education, 1989. In addition, the National Research Council Panel on Teacher Supply and Demand Models, of which one of the authors of this book (Murnane) was a member, commissioned detailed case studies of the recruitment, selection, and retention of science and mathematics teachers in six school districts chosen because they varied systematically in size, student clientele, enrollment trend, wealth, and location. The staff supporting the panel's activities also conducted "mini-case studies" in twenty-four other school districts through phone interviews with personnel directors and mail survey. Finally, the panel convened a conference of personnel directors from seven of the nation's largest school districts in order to discuss their recruiting and screening strategies. See further details in note 8.

5. These descriptions are based on Shivers, "Hiring Shortage-area and Non-shortage-area Teachers." The district names are pseudonyms.

6. Shivers, "Hiring Shortage-area and Non-shortage-area Teachers," p. 32.

7. Ibid., p. 44.

8. These case studies were conducted by staff members and consultants of the National Research Council's Panel on Statistics on Supply and Demand for Precollege Science and Mathematics Teachers. The case studies were initiated and guided by Dorothy M. Gilford, the study director of the panel. The consultants Jane L. David, Jennifer Pruyn, and Marianne Amarel conducted the case studies, using a common protocol, designed with advice from panel members, in California, Utah, and Maryland. Piggyback case studies were also conducted in twenty-four school districts across the country to explore the teacher supply-demand situation in the districts and were carried out by telephone and correspondence. Ellen Tenenbaum designed and carried out the piggyback studies. As a panel member, Richard Murnane gained valuable insights about teacher supply and demand at the school-district level from various activities carried out to obtain background for the panel's report and from discussions by panel members at the meetings. See also note 4.

9. Contract between the Boston Teacher Union and the School Committee of the City of Boston, 1990–1992, Boston, Mass.

5. *How Long Do Teachers Stay in Teaching?*

1. These projections are based on information provided by Howard Nelson at the American Federation of Teachers. He projected the percentages for 1994 and 2004 by using data from 1974 and 1984 and assuming that the attrition patterns for each age group would remain the same from decade to decade.
2. There were a sizable number of teachers in Michigan who taught part-time at various points in their careers. These teachers were much more likely to leave teaching than were full-time teachers. We conjecture that some of these terminations resulted from positions being eliminated, and were thus involuntary. Because this book focuses on voluntary behavior, and because we could not distinguish the voluntary from the involuntary terminations, we eliminated part-time teachers from our analyses.
3. As in Chapter 3, we examine the careers of those public school teachers in North Carolina who took the general and professional knowledge subtest of the NTE and held a continuing teaching license. This is not a subset of the North Carolina data set used in Chapter 3, however, in that we include here teachers who were licensed in 1974 and entered teaching within four years of licensure.
4. The last year for which we have data varies across the data sets. It is the 1984–85 school year in Michigan, and the 1985–86 school year in North Carolina.
5. For the Michigan database, we define subject-area specialty as the primary subject taught during the first year of teaching. In the North Carolina database, we know only the field of primary licensure. To simplify our discussion, we refer to this area of primary licensure for North Carolina teachers as their "subject-area specialty."
6. We have not treated moves between school districts within North Carolina and Michigan as exits from the profession. Moves out of state have been treated as exits, however, because as explained in Chapter 2, we do not know what happens to teachers who disappear from the state Department of Education records from which we built our Michigan and North Carolina data sets. In principle, we also know the first-spell length for every teacher in the NLS data sets. However, we found that the median first-spell length for these teachers was considerably shorter than the median first-spell length for either the Michigan or North Carolina samples. This seems implausible, given that a move from a teaching position in one state to a teaching position in another state would not be treated as the end of a first spell in these data. Consequently, we believe that the short spell lengths in the NLS data stem from limitations in these data and, in particular, to years in which no interviews were conducted and, consequently, no information on employment status is available.
7. Of the teachers in the Michigan sample, 31.5 percent were still teaching at the end of the period of observation, and of the teachers in the North Carolina sample, 53.2 percent.
8. See Appendix B for a description of our analytic methodology.
9. There are two hypotheses that seek to explain the declining hazard profile. The first, which economists call "state dependence," concerns reasons why "survival" of the first years of teaching might lead teachers to stay in the profession. The second, which economists call "heterogeneity," concerns differences between

teachers who stay in the classroom and those who leave. It would be useful to know which of these hypotheses is more important in terms of explaining our findings. For example, if "state dependence" is more important, then finding ways to help teachers survive the initial years in the classroom would result in significantly lower attrition. If "heterogeneity" is more important, then this policy would probably not be effective in reducing attrition because those teachers who leave teaching do so primarily because they had plans to pursue alternative occupations. Unfortunately, we cannot test the relative importance of these two hypotheses.

10. There were 387 (5.6 percent) Black teachers in the Michigan data set and 1,296 (13.4 percent) in the North Carolina data set.

11. Of the Black teachers in our Michigan sample, 48 percent began their careers in districts with enrollments of 16,000 or more; only 10 percent of the White teachers in our sample began their careers in such districts. Also, only 5 percent of the Black teachers began to teach in districts with enrollments of 2,500 or less; 35 percent of the White teachers began to teach in such districts.

12. In school districts in which Black teachers in North Carolina began their careers, 32 percent of the students were minority group members and 22 percent were poor. Corresponding figures for White teachers are 4 and 18.

13. Metropolitan Life Insurance Company, *Metropolitan Life Survey of the American Teacher* (New York: Metropolitan Life Insurance Company, 1988), p. 5.

14. We achieved this statistical control by incorporating dummy variables representing each school district as predictors in our hazard models—an approach that has been called the method of "fixed effects" elsewhere (see Appendix B). We use a similar strategy for identical reasons later in this chapter, when we examine the relationship between career duration and salary. For further discussion of the fixed-effects technique, see Richard J. Murnane and Randall J. Olsen, "The Effects of Salaries and Opportunity Costs on Length of Stay in Teaching: Evidence from North Carolina," *Journal of Human Resources,* 25, no. 1 (Winter 1990), 106–124.

15. See, for example, Richard J. Murnane and Barbara R. Phillips, "Learning by Doing, Vintage, and Selection: Three Pieces of the Puzzle Relating Teaching Experience and Teaching Performance," *Economics of Education Review,* 2 (1981), 453–465.

16. See Table 11 in James P. Smith and Finis R. Welch, "Black Economic Progress after Myrdal," *Journal of Economic Literature,* 27, no. 2 (June 1989), 519–564, at pp. 534–535.

17. Within each state, we also investigated the relationship between the risk of leaving teaching and demographic characteristics without controlling for subject-area specialty (that is, we repeated the analyses underlying Table 5.2 but we removed subject-area specialty from the model). Such analyses answer questions concerning which demographic group stays the longest, the shortest, and so forth among the stock of all teachers taken together.

The "uncontrolled" findings were essentially the same as the "controlled" findings. At every stage of their teaching careers, women who began teaching after the age of 30 were the least likely to leave the profession. In both states, median employment duration for mature women was longer than the entire period of data collection: 12 years in Michigan, and 11 years in North Carolina. We also found that, among teachers in Michigan, women who were younger on entry into teaching were much more likely to leave the profession than were men or mature women, as was the case when subject-area specialty was controlled. The median employment duration for younger women entering teaching in Michigan was 4.6 years, 2 to 8 years less than the median employment durations of the other demographic groups.

However, although younger women in Michigan were *consistently* at greater risk of leaving teaching in every year of their career than any other group, this is not entirely the case in North Carolina. In North Carolina, when subject-area specialty is uncontrolled, younger women were *less likely* to leave teaching than were their male counterparts for the first few years of their teaching career. But among younger women who stayed in teaching for at least five years, the risk of leaving in all subsequent years was higher than the risk associated with the other demographic groups. We believe that this early anomaly in the behavior of younger women teachers in North Carolina is largely attributable to between-state differences in the distribution of these women across the subject-area specialties. In North Carolina *more* younger women entered the *least* risky specialty (elementary school teaching, as we shall see later) than in Michigan, and *fewer* younger women entered the *most* risky high school specialties, thus accounting for the higher median career duration of younger women teachers in North Carolina.

18. All but 20 of the 437 women in the NLS data sets who entered teaching did so at the age of 30 or less. Consequently, the patterns we find in the NLS data refer exclusively to the group we call "younger women."

19. We replicated our analyses of subject-specific differences in career duration *uncontrolled* for the influence of entry age and gender. In North Carolina, the order and magnitude of subject-specific risks did not change when the demographic predictors were removed from the hazard model. In Michigan, however, the distribution of the age/gender groups across subject specialties had an important impact on the subject-specific risks of leaving teaching.

In North Carolina and in Michigan (with the exception of biology teachers), elementary school teachers were still the least likely to leave and therefore had considerably longer first spells than did secondary school teachers. In North Carolina, the median first-spell duration for elementary school teachers was more than 11 years and in Michigan it was 5.5 years. At the secondary school level, in both states, chemistry and physics teachers again had the highest risk of leaving and biology teachers were at a lower risk. Chemistry and physics teachers had particularly short median first-spell lengths (4.0 years in North Carolina and 2.9 years in Michigan); half of all biology teachers remained beyond the tenth year in Michigan and the sixth year in North Carolina.

These differences between the "controlled" and "uncontrolled" analyses are attributable to between-state differences in the age/gender mix across subject specialties. For example, young women—the demographic group in Michigan most likely to leave teaching—were overrepresented among elementary school teachers. Young women represented only 59 percent of the total sample, but 69 percent of the elementary school teachers. As a result, the effect of being a younger woman masqueraded, in part, as a subject-specialty effect. In the uncontrolled analysis, this made elementary school teaching appear more risky than it might otherwise have been if all demographic groups had been equally attracted to it. At the other extreme, biology was dominated by young men—who were less likely to leave teaching than young women. In the uncontrolled analysis, this appeared to make biology teaching less risky and biology teachers longer "lived."

20. Barbara Q. Beaudin, "Research Update IV: Differences in the Characteristics of New, Returning, and Migrating Teachers in Eight Subject Area Subgroups Hired in Connecticut's Public School Districts for the 1988–89 School Year," unpublished report, Connecticut State Department of Education, Hartford, Conn., 1989.

21. Other researchers have also reported a negative relationship between teachers' standardized test scores and length of stay in teaching. For example, see F. Howard Nelson, "New Perspectives on the Teacher Quality Debate: Empirical Evidence from the National Longitudinal Survey," *Journal of Educational Research*, 78, no. 3 (January/February 1985), 133–140; and Phillip C. Schlechty and Victor S. Vance, "Do Academically Able Teachers Leave Education? The North Carolina Case," *Phi Delta Kappan*, 63, no. 2 (October 1981), 106–112.

22. A test-score differential of a given size, say 100 points, is associated with a larger difference in five-year survival rates at the top of the NTE scale than at the bottom. Among White teachers, a difference of 97 points between the 10th and 50th percentiles corresponded to a 6-percentage-point difference in five-year survival, whereas a 100-point difference between the 50th and 90th percentiles corresponded to a 9-percentage-point difference. The reason is that both NTE score and the square of NTE score were included as predictors in our hazard models.

23. Table B.7, Model 5.14. We use the term "career duration" to refer to length of first spell.

24. Nelson, "New Perspectives on the Teacher Quality Debate."

25. Other recent studies support our finding that salaries affect teacher turnover. For example, see Nabeel Alsalam and Anne L. Hafner, "An Event Analysis of Entry, Exit, and Re-entry into the Teaching Profession: Evidence from the High School Class of 1972," paper presented at the meeting of the American Educational Research Association, Boston, Mass., April 1990; Bill D. Rickman and Carl D. Parker, "Alternative Wages and Teacher Mobility: A Human Capital Approach," *Economics of Education Review*, 9, no. 1 (1990), 73–79; and Russell W. Rumberger, The Impact of Salary Differentials on Teacher Shortages and Turnover: The Case of Mathematics and Science Teachers, *Economics of Education Review*, 6, no. 4 (1987), 389–399.

26. We constructed the average salary profile as follows: within each state, the initial salary was calculated as the average first-year salary paid by all school districts in the earliest year for which we have data (1972 in Michigan and 1974 in North Carolina) to teachers with a bachelor's degree and no prior teaching experience. The second-year salary was calculated as the average second-year salary paid by all school districts the following year (1973 in Michigan and 1975 in North Carolina), and so on.

27. In earlier work, we reported an even larger differential in median lifetimes associ-

ated with a $2,000 salary differential for White teachers in North Carolina. See Murnane and Olsen, "The Effects of Salaries and Opportunity Costs . . . Evidence from North Carolina," and Richard J. Murnane, Judith D. Singer, and John B. Willett, "The Influences of Salaries and 'Opportunity Costs' on Teachers' Career Choices: Evidence from North Carolina," *Harvard Educational Review*, 59, no. 3 (August 1989), 325–346. The difference in the estimates stems, to a large extent, from differences in sample definitions. The differential reported in this chapter is based on samples of White and Black teachers holding continuing licenses. The earlier differentials were based on a sample of White teachers including both continuing and provisional licensees. One reason the earlier differentials are larger is that teachers with provisional licenses tend to find jobs in school districts paying low salaries, and they tend to leave teaching after only one year in the classroom. We did not include the provisional licensees in the analysis in this chapter because it seemed likely that many of the provisionally licensed teachers left their jobs involuntarily, and we focus here on voluntary attrition. Exclusion of Black teachers from the samples used in the earlier papers also contributed to somewhat larger estimates of salary effects, because the point estimate of the impact of salary on the risk of leaving teaching is smaller for Black teachers than for White teachers. However, the difference between the estimates of the salary effect for Black teachers and White teachers is not statistically significant in either Michigan or North Carolina.

28. Only in Michigan was there a statistically significant difference between secondary and elementary school in the prediction of hazard by salary.

29. In Model 5.6 of Table B.5 and Model 5.13 of Table B.6, the interactions between salary and length of first spell are statistically significant and act to reduce the main effects of salary to zero for teachers with longer first spells.

30. Economists refer to the first type of explanation as "state dependence," and to the second type as "heterogeneity"; see note 9.

31. Data on the characteristics were obtained from the 1980 U.S. Census of Population, with the data mapped to school district boundaries.

32. For further discussion of the fixed effects technique, see Murnane and Olsen, "The Effects of Salaries and Opportunity Costs . . . Evidence from North Carolina," and Appendix B. We used this strategy to reexamine hazard as a function of all the predictors in our original hazards model (minus the district characteristics), by adding dummy variables to represent each school district.

33. Based on a model that included district characteristics, we estimate that 60 percent of North Carolina secondary school teachers paid at the median salary taught for more than five years, and that 64 percent of those paid at a salary $2,000 above the median salary taught for more than five years. The comparable numbers based on the fixed-effects estimation are 56 percent and 60 percent. Based on a model that included district characteristics, we estimate that 35 percent of Michigan secondary school teachers paid at the median salary taught for more than five years, and that 42 percent of those paid $2,000 above the median salary taught for more than five years. The comparable numbers for Michigan based on the fixed-effects estimation are 35 percent and 44 percent.

34. The results of our "district-specific" analyses are compatible with the results

reported earlier in the chapter concerning the relative lengths of Black teachers' and White teachers' careers. We reported that Black teachers are more likely than White teachers to start their careers in large urban districts where working conditions are difficult, and career durations are relatively short. It is also the case that salaries in these districts tend to be relatively high. As a result, the average starting salary for Black teachers in each state (expressed in 1988 dollars) is higher than the starting salary for White teachers. In Michigan, the average starting salary is $22,858 for Black teachers and $22,294 for White teachers. The comparable salaries for North Carolina teachers are $18,220 and $18,181.

6. Who Returns to Teaching?

1. Beverly Kempton, "Great Transformations: How Four Teachers Changed Careers and Changed Their Lives," *Working Woman,* 14 (January 1989), 89–92.
2. Kay Scheidler, "Exploring the Myths: Why I Left High Tech and Returned to Teaching," *Teacher's Journal,* 1, no. 1 (Spring 1988), 11–14, at p. 11.
3. Ibid., p. 14.
4. Information provided by the Connecticut State Department of Education, 1987.
5. Unpublished table provided by John Stiglmeier, Director of the Information Center on Education, New York State Education Department, 1987.
6. James Bryant Conant, *The Education of American Teachers* (New York: McGraw-Hill, 1963), p. 229.
7. National Education Association, *Status of the American Public School Teacher: 1985–86* (Washington, D.C.: NEA, 1987).
8. The reframing of our research question from "Who returns" to "How long do they stay out?" permits us to deal with the censoring that is a problematic component of this type of analysis (see Appendix B).
9. As explained in note 6 of Chapter 5, we question the reliability of the information on first-spell lengths and career interruptions in the NLS data set. The problem stems from years in which participants were not interviewed and consequently no information on occupational status is available. For this reason, we rely most heavily on the state-specific databases in describing who returns to teaching, and use the NLS only to describe the role of occupational status during the career interruption.
10. Based on raw frequencies from the NLS Young Women, Young Men, and Youth surveys, sampling weights not included.
11. Table B.9, Model 6.2, and Table B.10, Model 6.5.
12. Frank Levy and Richard C. Michel, "Education and Income: Recent U.S. Trends," paper prepared for the Joint Economic Committee of the U.S. Congress, December 1988, pp. 13–14.
13. In Michigan, age at end of first spell was a more important predictor of the probability that a former teacher would return to the classroom than gender was. The explanation, we believe, is that age is closely correlated with seniority, and teachers' contracts state that, if teachers are laid off as a result of declining enrollments, those with the most seniority will be the first to be rehired. This hypothesis is supported by evidence that length of first spell is a more important predictor

of the probability of a return to teaching in Michigan, where large enrollment declines took place, than in North Carolina, where student enrollments were quite stable.

14. A second reason for the relatively high return probability for elementary school teachers is that women, who are more likely to return to teaching than men, are more heavily represented among elementary school teachers than among secondary school teachers. Even when estimated in the context of a model that held constant the influence of age and gender, however, elementary school teachers were still the subject group with the highest probability of returning to teaching.

15. Table B.10, Model 6.7.

7. Revising Licensing Requirements

1. See Simon Rottenberg, ed., *Occupational Licensure and Regulation* (Washington, D.C.: American Enterprise Institute for Public Policy Research, 1980), p. 2.

2. For a discussion of how licensing requirements hinder innovation in the design of medical school curricula, see Lee S. Shulman, "Reconnecting Foundations to the Substance of Teacher Education," *Teachers College Record*, 91, no. 3 (Spring 1990), 300–310.

3. For a description of traditional state requirements for teacher licensure, see Arthur E. Wise and Linda Darling-Hammond, *Licensing Teachers: Design for a Teaching Profession* (Santa Monica, Calif.: RAND Corporation, 1987), pp. 12–14.

4. Lawrence M. Rudner and Thomas E. Eissenberg, "State Testing of Teachers: The 1989 Report," Eric Clearinghouse on Tests, Measurement, and Evaluation, Digest EDO-TM-89-10, American Institutes for Research, Washington, D.C., December 1989.

5. See F. Howard Nelson, "New Perspectives on the Teacher Quality Debate: Empirical Evidence from the National Longitudinal Survey," *Journal of Educational Research*, 78, no. 3 (January/February 1985), 133–140. Another contributing factor, which we discuss in Chapter 8, may be differences in working conditions.

6. Donna H. Kerr, "Teaching Competence and Teacher Education in the United States," *Teachers College Record*, 84, no. 3 (Spring 1983), 525–552. It should be pointed out that no well-controlled quantitative study of the effects of teacher education on subsequent teaching performance has ever been conducted.

7. *Guidelines for Proper Use of NTE Tests* (Princeton, N.J.: Educational Testing Service, 1988). The number of NTE specialty-area tests was tallied from a table entitled "NTE Programs: Table of User Qualifying Scores and Validity Study Status Information," dated February 12, 1990, provided by Carol Dwyer of Educational Testing Service.

8. Rudner and Eissenberg, "State Testing of Teachers." Thirteen states require applicants for a teaching license to take both the NTE Core Battery and an NTE specialty-area test.

9. G. Pritchie Smith, *The Effects of Competency Testing on the Supply of Minority Teachers*, report prepared for the National Education Association and the Council of Chief State School Officers, Jacksonville, Fla., December 1987.

10. Walt Haney, George Madaus, and Amelia Kreitzer, "Charms Talismanic: Testing Teachers for the Improvement of American Education," *Review of Research in Education,* 14 (1987), 169–238. Quotation is from page 199.

11. Rudner and Eissenberg, "State Testing of Teachers."

12. See Wise and Darling-Hammond, *Licensing Teachers,* p. 22.

13. *From Gatekeeper to Gateway: Transforming Testing in America,* report of the National Commission on Testing and Public Policy (Chestnut Hill, Mass.: Boston College, 1990), p. 28.

14. Joan C. Baratz, "Black Participation in the Teacher Pool," paper prepared for the Task Force on Teaching as a Profession, Carnegie Forum on Education and the Economy, January 1986, pp. 29–31.

15. *South Carolina,* 445 F.Supp. 1094 (D.S.C. 1977, *aff'd,* 434 U.S. 1026 (1978), 1108, as cited in Judith H. Cohen, "Legal Challenges to Testing for Teacher Certification: History, Impact, and Future Trends," *Journal of Law and Education,* 18, no. 2 (Spring 1989), 229–265. Quotation is from page 241.

16. Samuel H. Preston, "Children and the Elderly: Divergent Paths for America's Dependents," *Demography,* 21 (1984), 435–457.

17. For example, see Joseph Berger, "New York Schools and Patronage: Experience Teaches Hard Lessons," *New York Times,* December 11, 1989, p. 1.

18. John H. Bishop, "Is the Test Score Decline Responsible for the Productivity Growth Decline?" *American Economic Review,* 79, no. 1 (March 1989), 178–197.

19. See Robert H. Haveman and Barbara L. Wolfe, "Education, Productivity, and Well-Being: On Defining and Measuring the Economic Characteristics of Schooling," in *Education and Economic Productivity,* ed. Edwin Dean (Cambridge, Mass.: Ballinger, 1984).

20. *New Jersey Provisional Teacher Program: Handbook for State-Approved District Training and Supervision Programs* (Trenton, N.J.: New Jersey State Department of Education, July 1989), p. 1.

21. Ibid.

22. "Provisional Teacher Program: Information for Applicants," New Jersey State Department of Education, Trenton, N.J., 1989.

23. *The Provisional Teacher Program: Fifth-Year Report* (Princeton, N.J.: New Jersey State Department of Education, December 1989), p. 6. Hereafter cited as *Fifth-Year Report.*

24. Ibid., p. 4.

25. Ibid., p. 15.

26. Ibid., p. 12.

27. Another element of a successful strategy for recruiting minority group members to teaching may be financial aid. The New Jersey Department of Education aggressively recruits minority candidates to the Provisional Teacher Program and provides scholarship aid to the most promising candidates (*Fifth-Year Report,* p. 12).

28. *Fifth-Year Report,* p. 14.

29. C. Emily Feistritzer, *Alternative Teacher Certification: A State-by-State Analysis, 1990* (Washington, D.C.: National Center for Education Information, 1990).

30. Kenneth Carlson et al., "An Analysis of the Proposal by the New Jersey Education Department for an Alternative Route to Teacher Certification," unpublished paper, Rutgers University, Graduate School of Education, November 15, 1983.

31. Lee S. Shulman, "Knowledge and Teaching: Foundations of the New Reform," *Harvard Educational Review,* 57, no. 1 (February 1987), 1–22. Quotation is from page 15.

32. Ibid., p. 7.

33. Ibid., p. 20.

34. See Pamela L. Grossman, "Learning to Teach without Teacher Education," *Teachers College Record,* 91, no. 2 (Winter 1989), 191–208, and Pamela L. Grossman, "A Study in Contrast: Sources of Pedagogical Content Knowledge for Secondary English," *Journal of Teacher Education,* 40, no. 5 (September/October 1989), 24–31.

35. The number of states using tests of subject knowledge as part of teaching licensing procedures is reported in Rudner and Eissenberg, "State Testing of Teachers."

36. Jerome Pine, "Validity of Science Assessments," in *The Assessment of Hands-on Elementary Science Programs,* ed. George Hein (Grand Forks, N.D.: Center for Teaching and Learning, University of North Dakota, August 1990), pp. 83–94. Pine's analysis was conducted as part of the work of the National Research Council Committee on improving indicators of the quality of precollege math and science education. For a description of the committee's findings, see Richard J. Murnane and Senta Raizen, *Improving Indicators of the Quality of Science and Mathematics Education in Grades K–12* (Washington, D.C.: National Academy Press, 1988).

37. *Toward High and Rigorous Standards for the Teaching Profession* (Washington, D.C.: National Board for Professional Teaching Standards, July 1989).

38. For a description of the NBPTS research agenda, see Joan Baratz-Snowden, "The NBPTS Begins Its Research and Development Program," *Educational Researcher,* 19, no. 6 (August/September 1990), 19–24.

39. The three strategies we describe by no means exhaust the types of approaches to performance assessment. Later in this chapter we describe one alternative, currently being implemented by the state of Connecticut. For a thoughtful approach to assessing the skills of laboratory science teachers, see Patricia Wheeler and Janelle Page, *Development of a Science Laboratory Assessment for New Teachers, Grades K–12: California New Teacher Project,* vol. 1, Final Report (Mountain View, Calif.: RMC Research Corporation, June 29, 1990).

40. Stephen Klein, Linda Darling-Hammond, Tamar Gendler, and Arthur Wise, "Developing a Prototype Licensing Examination for Secondary School English Teachers," a proposal submitted to the State of California Commission on Teacher Credentialing, (n.d.), p. 2.

41. *Working Papers toward A New Generation of Teacher Assessments* (Princeton, N.J.: Educational Testing Service, January 1990).

42. See Carol Anne Dwyer and Ana Maria Villegas, "Assessing the Beginning Teacher: Guiding Conceptions," unpublished paper, Educational Testing Service, Princeton, N.J., July 1990.

43. Allan Collins and John Frederiksen, "Five Traits of Good Teaching: Learning, Thinking, Listening, Involving, Helping," unpublished report, Bolt, Baranek, and Newman Laboratories, Inc., Cambridge, Mass., 1989.

44. See Klein et al., "Developing a Prototype," p. 8.

45. For other problems with performance assessments, see ibid.

46. Allan Collins expressed this point of view in a personal communication.

47. For a discussion of "systemic validity," see John R. Frederiksen and Allan Collins, "A Systems Approach to Educational Testing," *Educational Researcher*, 18, no. 9 (December 1989), 27–32.

48. U.S. Bureau of the Census, *Statistical Abstract of the United States: 1990*, 110th ed. (Washington, D.C.: U.S. Department of Commerce, 1990), p. 437.

49. The estimate of the average starting salary for U.S. teachers for the 1987–88 school year was provided by the National Education Association. See note 19 of Chapter 1 for an alternate estimate.

50. "Research Bulletin no. 4, School Year 1989–1990," Division of Research, Evaluation and Assessment, Connecticut State Department of Education, 1990.

51. *Connecticut Enrollment Projections to the Year 2005* (Hartford, Conn.: Bureau of Research and Teacher Assessment, Division of Research, Evaluation and Assessment, Connecticut State Department of Education, 1989).

52. Applicants may also satisfy the basic skills requirement by submitting scores above prespecified cutoffs on the Prueba de Aptitud Académica.

53. An exception is candidates for a license to teach elementary education. These candidates take a test designed by the Connecticut Department of Education.

54. The information on cutscores in different states comes from a table entitled "NTE Programs: Table of User Qualifying Scores and Validity Study Status Information," dated February 12, 1990, provided by Carol Dwyer of Educational Testing Service.

55. See Mitchell Chester and Cynthia Jorgenson, "BEST Assessment Program Implemented," *UPDATE: Cooperative Teacher Program—Beginning Education Support and Training Program: Support and Assessment* (Hartford, Conn.: Connecticut State Department of Education, Summer 1989).

56. The Connecticut Department of Education has plans to develop assessment centers at which the skills of candidates for teaching licenses would be examined. This may complement or replace the current system of evaluations by trained assessors.

57. Raymond L. Pecheone and Neil B. Carey, "The Validity of Performance Assessment for Teacher Licensure: Connecticut's Ongoing Research," *Journal of Personnel Evaluation in Education*, 3 (1990), 115–142. Quotation is from page 121.

58. For a thoughtful discussion of the difficulties of reforming U.S. education through governmental policies, see Richard F. Elmore and Milbrey W. McLaughlin, *Steady Work* (Santa Monica, Calif.: RAND Corporation, 1988).

59. See *The Alternate Route to Teacher Certification* (Hartford, Conn.: Connecticut Department of Higher Education, 1990).

60. The passing rates were provided by Pascal D. Forgione, Jr., Director of the Division of Research, Evaluation and Assessment, Connecticut State Department of Education.

61. This statistic was provided by the Office for Educational Research and Improvement, U.S. Department of Education.

62. The figure of 3 percent was computed from data in Table 20 of *The CONNCEPT Program: A Four-Year Report* (Hartford, Conn.: Connecticut State Department of Education, 1990), p. 44.

63. See *The CONNCEPT Program: A Four-Year Report.*

64. The Alternate Route Program in Connecticut is still too new and too small to provide information on whether a significant number of Black college graduates who could pass the CONNCEPT will be attracted to a teaching program that does not require undergraduate preparation.

8. Getting the Incentives Right

1. *Toward High and Rigorous Standards for the Teaching Profession* (Washington, D.C.: National Board for Professional Teaching Standards, July 1989), p. 34.

2. Eric A. Hanushek, "The Economics of Schooling," *Journal of Economic Literature,* 24, no. 3 (September 1986), 1141–1177. See especially page 1161.

3. National Education Association, *Status of the American Public School Teacher: 1985–86* (Washington, D.C.: NEA, 1987), p. 72.

4. Philip W. Jackson, *Life in Classrooms* (New York: Holt, Rinehart, and Winston, 1968).

5. The material in this section draws heavily from Richard J. Murnane and David K. Cohen, "Merit Pay and the Evaluation Problem: Why Most Merit Pay Plans Fail and a Few Survive," *Harvard Educational Review,* 56, no. 1 (1986), 1–17.

6. See Charles F. Manski, "Academic Ability, Earnings, and the Decision to Become a Teacher: Evidence from the National Longitudinal Study of the High School Class of 1972," in *Public Sector Payrolls,* ed. David A. Wise (Chicago, Ill.: University of Chicago Press, 1987), pp. 291–312; and Peter Dolton, "The Economics of UK Teacher Supply: The Graduate's Decision," *Economic Journal,* 100, no. 4 (1990), 91–104.

7. David Monk and Stephen Jacobson, "The Distribution of Salary Increments between Veteran and Novice Teachers: Evidence from New York State," *Journal of Education Finance,* 11 (1985), 157 - 175.

8. Richard J. Murnane, Judith D. Singer, and John B. Willett, "Changes in Teacher Salaries during the 1970s: The Role of School District Demographics," *Economics of Education Review,* 6, no. 4 (1987), 379–388.

9. Richard J. Murnane and Barbara R. Phillips, "What Do Effective Teachers of Inner City Children Have in Common?" *Social Science Research,* 10 (1981), 83–100; and Richard J. Murnane, *The Impact of School Resources on the Learning of Inner City Children* (Cambridge, Mass.: Ballinger, 1975).

10. Contract between the Boston Teacher Union and the School Committee of the City of Boston, 1990–1992, Boston, Mass.

11. Agreement between the Board of Education of the School District of the City of Detroit (Mich.) and the Detroit Federation of Teachers, Local 231, American Federation of Teachers, AFL-CIO, July 1, 1987–June 30, 1990; Agreement be-

tween the Hartford (Conn.) Federation of Teachers and the Hartford Board of Education, effective July 1, 1985–June 30, 1989.

12. *The Revolution That Is Overdue,* report of the AFT Task Force on the Future of Education (Washington, D.C.: American Federation of Teachers, 1986).

13. Susan Moore Johnson, *Teachers at Work* (New York: Basic Books, 1990).

14. Lorraine M. McDonnell and Milbrey W. McLaughlin, *Program Consolidation and the State Role in ESEA Title IV* (Santa Monica, Calif.: RAND Corporation, 1980).

15. The occupational choice figures were calculated from the data in the NLS file that we constructed.

16. See H. W. More and P. C. Unsinger, eds., *The Policy Assessment Center* (Springfield, Ill.: Charles C. Thomas, 1987), as cited in Raymond L. Pecheone and Neil B. Carey, "The Validity of Performance Assessment for Teacher Licensure: Connecticut's Ongoing Research," *Journal of Personnel Evaluation in Education,* 3 (1990), 115–142.

Appendix A. Research Context

1. More detailed information on the Michigan and North Carolina databases is available in: (1) the *Michigan Codebook,* prepared by James Kemple, Michael Schwinden, and Dennis Sweeney (1989), and (2) the *North Carolina Codebook,* prepared by James Kemple and Michael Schwinden (1989). Both of these unpublished documents and the data sets themselves are available from the Interuniversity Consortium for Political and Social Research (ICPSR), Ann Arbor, Michigan.

2. Further information on the national database is available in the *NLS Codebook* prepared by Anne Chase and Beth Gamse (1990). This unpublished document and the data set are available from ICPSR. In addition, a document entitled *NLS Handbook,* describing all of the NLS datasets, is available at no charge from the Center for Human Resource Research, Ohio State University.

3. The racial composition of the 1981 North Carolina teaching force was provided by M. Engin Konanc, the director of the Information Center, North Carolina Department of Education. He stated that 1981 is the earliest year for which the racial composition of the North Carolina teaching force is available.

4. We computed the starting salaries in North Carolina from a database that was constructed from paper copies of the North Carolina school district salary schedules for each year from 1976 to 1986. The estimate of the average starting salary in the nation was provided by the National Education Association. The competitiveness of North Carolina teaching salaries with respect to the rest of the country varies considerably from year to year. North Carolina salaries were particularly competitive in 1980 because the state legislature dramatically increased the state scale in the previous year. The average salary for beginning teachers in North Carolina was 4 percent above the national average in 1978 and 3 percent above the national average in 1986. Notice that the teacher salary figures reported in Appendix A are expressed in 1980 dollars to make them comparable with the per capita income figures displayed in Table A.1. Other salary figures reported in the text are expressed in 1988 dollars.

5. Since teachers' contracts in most school districts specify that involuntary transfers and layoffs are based on seniority, teachers who start their careers when enrollments are stable are less vulnerable to involuntary job changes than are teachers who start to teach during periods of declining enrollment.

6. A preliminary examination of the data indicated that teaching careers were substantially shorter among teachers who began their careers in the late 1970s and the early 1980s compared with those of teachers who started to teach in the early and mid-1970s. We conjectured that involuntary teacher layoffs caused by decreasing enrollments were the most likely explanation. One could argue, however, that teachers hired during the early 1970s could foresee the enrollment declines that were to come in the late 1970s, and consequently adjusted their career decisions in anticipation of the influences the declines would have on their career options. If this is the case, then the career paths of Michigan teachers in the 1970s may not be representative of the career paths to be expected among teachers during the 1990s, when enrollments are expected to rise in most parts of the country (see Gary Zarkin, "Occupational Choice: An Application to the Market for Public School Teachers," *Quarterly Journal of Economics*, 100, no. 2 (May 1985), 409–446, for a discussion of this point). Without minimizing the potential impact of enrollment declines on teachers' career paths in the 1970s, however, it is striking that our findings are so similar, whether it is the career paths of teachers in Michigan or in North Carolina (where student enrollments were more stable) that are being studied.

Appendix B. Methodology

1. For further information on the variables that were used in our analyses, see the following: (1) the *Michigan Codebook*, prepared by James Kemple, Michael Schwinden, and Dennis Sweeney (1989), (2) the *North Carolina Codebook*, prepared by James Kemple and Michael Schwinden (1989), and (3) the *NLS Codebook*, prepared by Anne Chase and Beth Gamse (1990). All three of these unpublished documents are available from the Interuniversity Consortium for Political and Social Research (ICPSR), Ann Arbor, Michigan.

2. John B. Willett and Judith D. Singer, "Two Types of Questions about Time: Methodological Issues in the Analysis of Teacher Career Path Data," *International Journal of Educational Research*, 13, no. 4 (1989), 421–437.

3. P. D. Allison, *Event History Analysis: Regression for Longitudinal Event Data*, Sage University Paper Series on Quantitative Applications in the Social Sciences, series number 07–046 (Beverly Hills, Calif.: Sage Publications, 1984); J. D. Kalbfleisch and R. L. Prentice, *The Statistical Analysis of Failure Time Data* (New York: John Wiley, 1980).

4. Careful definitions of the hazard function distinguish duration measured *discretely*, for which hazard is a *conditional probability*, and duration measured *continuously*, for which hazard is a *rate*. See John B. Willett and Judith D. Singer, "How Long Did It Take . . .?: Using Survival Analysis in Educational and Psychological Research," in Linda M. Collins and John L. Horn, *Best Methods for the Analysis of Change* (Washington, D.C.: American Psychological Association, February, 1991).

5. P. D. Allison, "Discrete-Time Methods for the Analysis of Event Histories," in *Sociological Methodology,* ed. S. Leinhardt (San Francisco, Calif.: Jossey-Bass, 1982), pp. 61–98; B. Efron, "Logistic Regression, Survival Analysis, and the Kaplan-Meier Curve," *Journal of the American Statistical Association,* 83 (1988), 414–425; N. Laird and O. Oliver, "Covariance Analysis of Censored Survival Data Using Log-linear Analysis Techniques," *Journal of the American Statistical Association,* 76 (1981), 231–240.

6. Willett and Singer, "How Long Did It Take?"

7. For further discussion of the fixed-effects technique, see Richard J. Murnane and Randall J. Olsen, "The Effects of Salaries and Opportunity Costs on Length of Stay in Teaching: Evidence from North Carolina," *Journal of Human Resources,* 25, no. 1 (Winter 1990), 106–124.

8. See Allison, "Discrete-Time Methods for the Analysis of Event Histories."

Index

Ability, 9–11, 31, 35–36, 37, 85, 127–128
Achievement, student, 6, 7, 10, 49
Administrators, 49–53
Age, 24–27, 43–44, 101, 172n13; and career duration, 59, 60, 65–67, 168n17
Alternate Route Program, 112–113, 177n64
Alternative training programs, 90, 95–97, 99–102, 112–114, 125
American Federation of Teachers (AFT), 122, 167n1
Applicant pool. *See* Personnel pool
Assessment, 11, 16–17, 101–114, 119; performance-based, 102–114, 119, 129; alternative approaches, 105–114
Attrition, teacher, 59, 61–63, 66, 97, 122

"Baby boom," 19, 86
"Baby bust," 19, 46, 86
Bachelor's degree, 56, 93, 95, 116
Base salary, 5–6. *See also* Starting salary
Basic skills, tests of, 16, 91
Beginning Educator Support and Training (BEST) Program, 111
Beginning teachers. *See* Novice teachers
Biology teachers, 28, 69, 127, 170n19. *See also* Mathematics and science teachers
Blacks, 130, 134; expanded opportunities for, 5, 12, 33, 65, 128, 129; and career choice, 32–33, 91–93. *See also* Minorities; Race
Black teachers, 1, 10, 11–13, 108, 128–130; and test scores, 4, 12, 17, 21–24, 32–33, 70, 91–93, 113, 128–129,

165n21; and licensing, 12, 13, 17, 21–24, 31–33, 38–42, 91–93, 113–114; and urban school districts, 13, 63–64, 108, 123, 129, 147; and career duration, 60, 63–65, 70, 147
"Board Certification" status, 16, 104–105
Boston (Mass.) teachers' contract, 55–56, 57, 122
Boyer, Ernest, 10
Business and industry, 2, 67, 68; salaries in, 6, 8–9, 20, 46, 67, 69, 84, 127
Business education, 28, 29, 44

California, 105, 115
California Achievement Test, 91
Career choice, 4–5, 10, 13, 30–47, 69, 86, 138–143; of minorities, 5, 12, 29, 32–33; factors in, 5–13, 19–21, 69; and subject specialties, 27–29, 44–46; trends in, 31–46, 89–90; of women, 33, 43–44
Career duration, 9, 14, 43, 59–76, 143–153, 179n6; salaries and, 7, 60, 71–75, 119–120, 126, 170n25; gender and, 43, 65–67, 168–169n17; race and, 60, 63–65, 70; subject specialty and, 60, 67–69; test scores and, 60, 69–71, 170n21; age and, 65–67
Career mobility, teacher, 77. *See also* Return to teaching
Carnegie Forum on Education and the Economy, 2
Carnegie Task Force on Teaching as a Profession, 16, 104
Censoring, 60, 143–144